"[SYD FIELD IS THE] GURU OF WOULD-BE SCREENWRITERS. . . . SCREENPLAY IS THEIR BESTSELLING BIBLE."
—*Los Angeles Herald Examiner*

Syd Field

SCREENPLAY

"The basics of the craft in terms simple enough to enable any beginner to develop an idea into a submittable script."
—*American Cinematographer*

"A much-needed book . . . straightforward and informed . . . Facts and figures on markets, production details, layout of script, the nuts and bolts, are accurate and clear, and should be enormously helpful to novices."
—*Fade-In*

"[Syd Field is] the most sought-after screenwriting teacher in the world."
—*The Hollywood Reporter*

"Experienced advice on story development, creation and definition of characters, structure of action, and a direction of participants. Easy-to-follow guidelines and a commonsense approach mark this highly useful manual."
—*Video*

"Impressive because of its rare combinations: a technical book, apparently mechanically sound, that's quite personable and lively and also seems to care about us, about our doing things right and making good. His easy-to-follow, step-by-step approaches are comforting and his emphasis on right attitude and motivation is uplifting."
—*Los Angeles Times Book Review*

"Quite simply the *only* manual to be taken seriously by aspiring screenwriters."
—Tony Bill, co-producer of *The Sting*, director of *My Bodyguard*

"The complete primer, a step-by-step guide from the first glimmer of an idea to marketing the finished script."
—*New West*

"Full of common sense, an uncommon commodity."
—*Esquire*

"A much-needed book."
—Frank Pierson, Academy Award–winning screenwriter, President, Writers Guild of America West

Books by Syd Field:

The Screenwriter's Workbook

Screenplay: The Foundations of Screenwriting

Selling a Screenplay: The Screenwriter's Guide to Hollywood

Four Screenplays

The Screenwriter's Problem Solver:

How to recognize, identify, and define screenwriting

problems

Screenplay

The Foundations of Screenwriting

Syd Field

Expanded Edition

A DELL TRADE PAPERBACK

A DELL TRADE PAPERBACK
Published by
Dell Publishing
a division of
Bantam Doubleday Dell Publishing Group, Inc.
1540 Broadway
New York, New York 10036

ACKNOWLEDGMENTS
Grateful acknowledgment is made for permission to use the following.
From *Network* by Paddy Chayefsky: Printed by permission of Simcha
Productions, Inc. Copyright © Simcha Productions, Inc., 1976. Colin
Higgins for excerpt from the screenplay of *Silver Streak*. McDonald's
Corporation for "Press On," the motto of McDonald's Corporation.
"Sitting" by Cat Stevens: © 1972 Freshwater Music Ltd.—London,
England. All rights for U.S.A. and Canada controlled by Ackee Music,
Inc. (ASCAP). All rights reserved. Used by permission. Robert Towne for
excerpt from the screenplay of *Chinatown*.

ISBN: 0-440-57647-4
Reprinted by arrangement with Delacorte Press
Printed in the United States of America

July 1984

30 29

BVG

To the students,
writers and
readers of
the screenplay
—everywhere

A SPECIAL THANKS—

to all my students and the staff
at Sherwood Oaks Experimental College;
and to
Robert Towne, Paddy Chayefsky and
Colin Higgins;
and a
Special Acknowledgment
to Werner—
and all the people in *est*
who gave me the space, the opportunity,
and the support to grow and expand enough
to write this book—

Contents

To the reader:

My task . . . is to make you hear, to
make you feel—and, above all, to make
you *see*. That is all, and it is everything.

Joseph Conrad
Preface to
The Nigger of the Narcissus

Introduction

Wherein we discuss the origins of this book:

As a writer-producer for David L. Wolper Productions, a free-lance screenwriter, and head of the story department at Cinemobile Systems, I spent several years writing and reading screenplays. At Cinemobile alone, I read and synopsized more than 2,000 screenplays in a little more than two years. And of those 2,000 screenplays, I selected only 40 to present to our financial partners for possible film production.

Why so few? Because 99 out of 100 screenplays I read weren't good enough to invest a million or more dollars in. Or, put another way, only one out of 100 screenplays I read was good enough to consider for film production. And, at Cinemobile, our job was making movies. In one year alone, we were directly involved in the production of some 119 motion pictures, ranging from *The Godfather* to *Jeremiah Johnson* to *Deliverance*.

Cinemobile Systems provides location services to the film-maker, and has offices around the world. In Los Angeles alone, a fleet of 22 Cinemobiles serves the film and TV industry. Each unit is about the size of a Greyhound bus and is a compact, portable "studio" on wheels that supplies all the necessary camera equipment to make a movie. That includes all lights, generators, cameras, lenses, and a driver who is specially trained to handle 90 percent of the problems that arise on locations. It's an enormous amount of equipment, and it allows the cast and crew to jump into a unit and literally take off to make a movie.

When my boss, Fouad Said; the creator of the Cinemobile, decided to make his own movies, he went out and raised some $10 million in a few weeks. Pretty soon everybody in Hollywood was sending him screenplays. Thousands of scripts came in, from stars and directors, studios and producers, from the known and unknown.

That's when I was fortunate enough to be given the opportunity of reading the submitted screenplays, and evaluating them in terms of quality, cost, and probable budget. My job, as I was constantly reminded, was to "find material" for our three financial partners: the United Artists Theatre Group, the Hemdale Film Distribution Company, headquartered in London, and the Taft Broadcasting Company, parent company of Cinemobile.

So I began reading screenplays. As a former screenwriter taking a much-needed vacation from more than seven years of free-lance writing, my job at Cinemobile gave me a totally new perspective on writing screenplays. It was a tremendous opportunity, a formidable challenge, and a dynamic learning experience.

What made the 40 screenplays I recommended "better" than the others? I didn't have any answers for that, but I thought about it for a long time.

My reading experience gave me the opportunity to make a judgment and evaluation, to formulate an opinion: This is a *good* screenplay, this is *not a good* screenplay. As a screenwriter, I wanted to find out what made the 40 scripts I recommended better than the other 1,960 scripts submitted.

Just about this time I was given the opportunity of teaching a screenwriting class at the Sherwood Oaks Experimental College in Hollywood, now unfortunately out of business. Sherwood Oaks was a professional school taught by professionals. It was the kind of school where Paul Newman, Dustin Hoffman, and Lucille Ball gave acting seminars; where Tony Bill would teach a producing seminar; where Martin Scorsese, Robert Altman, or Alan Pakula gave directing seminars; where William Fraker and John Alonzo, two of the finest cinematographers in the world, taught a class in cinematography. It was a school where professional production managers, cameramen, film editors, writers, directors, and producers all came to teach their specialties. It was the most unique film school in the country.

I had never taught a screenwriting class before, so I had to delve into my writing experience and reading experience to evolve my basic material.

What is a good screenplay, I kept asking myself. And, pretty soon, I started getting some answers. When you read a good screenplay, you know it—it's evident from page one. The style, the way the words are laid out on the page, the way the story is set up, the grasp of dramatic situation, the introduction of the main character, the basic premise or problem of the screenplay—it's all set up in the first few pages of the script. *Chinatown, Three Days of the Condor, All the President's Men,* are perfect examples.

A screenplay, I soon realized, is a story told with pictures. It's like a *noun:* That is, a screenplay is about a *person,* or persons, in a *place,* or places, doing his, or her, *"thing."* I saw that the screenplay has certain basic conceptual components common to the form.

These elements are expressed dramatically within a definite structure with a beginning, middle, and end. When I reexamined the 40 screenplays submitted to our partners—

including *The Wind and the Lion, Alice Doesn't Live Here Anymore,* and others—I realized they all contained these basic concepts, regardless of how they were cinematically executed. They are in every screenplay.

I began teaching this conceptual approach to writing the screenplay. If the student knows what a model screenplay is, I reasoned, it can be used as a guide or blueprint.

I've been teaching this screenwriting class for several years now. It's an effective and experiential approach to writing the screenplay. My material has evolved and been formulated by thousands and thousands of students all over the world. They are the ones who prepared me to write this book.

Many of my students have been very successful: Anna Hamilton Phelan wrote *Mask* in my workshop, then went on to write *Gorillas in the Mist;* Laura Esquival wrote *Like Water for Chocolate;* Carmen Culver wrote *The Thorn Birds;* Janus Cercone wrote *Leap of Faith;* Linda Elsted won the prestigious Humanitas award for *The Divorce Wars;* and prestigious filmmakers such as James Cameron *(Terminator* and *Terminator 2: Judgment Day)* used the material when they started their careers. Screenwriting is a process. What you write one day is out of date the day after. What you write the day after is out of date the day after that. And what you write the day after the day after is out of date the day after that. That's just the way the writing process works; it is larger than you are. It has its own life, its own needs, its own requirements.

Others have not been so successful. Some people have talent, and some don't. Talent is God's gift; either you've got it, or you don't.

Many people have already formed a writing style prior to enrolling in the class. Some of them have to *unlearn* their writing habits, just as a tennis pro coaches someone to correct an incorrct swing, or a swimming instructor improves a swimming stroke. Writing, like tennis, or learning to swim, is an experiential process; for that reason, I begin with general concepts and then move into specific aspects of screenwriting.

The material is designed for everyone; for those who have no previous writing experience, as well as those who have not had much success with their writing efforts and need to rethink their basic approach to writing. Novelists, playwrights, magazine editors, housewives, businessmen, doctors, actors, film editors, commercial directors, secretaries, advertising executives, and university professors—all have taken the class and benefited from it.

The purpose of this book is to enable the reader to sit down and write a screenplay from the position of choice, confidence, and security; completely secure within himself that he knows what he's doing. Because the hardest thing about writing is *knowing what to write.*

When you complete this book, you will know exactly *what* to do to write a screenplay. Whether you do it or not is up to you.

Writing is a personal responsibility—either you do it, or you don't.

1

What Is a Screenplay?

Wherein we introduce the paradigm *of dramatic structure:*

What is a screenplay? A guide, or an outline for a movie? A blueprint, or diagram? A series of images, scenes, and sequences that are strung together with dialogue and description, like pearls on a strand? The landscape of a dream? A collection of ideas? What *is* a screenplay? Well, for one thing it's not a novel, and it's certainly not a play.

If you look at a novel and try to define its essential nature, you see that the dramatic action, the story line, usually takes place inside the head of the main character. We are privy to the character's thoughts, feelings, words, actions, memories, dreams, hopes, ambitions, opinions, and more. If other characters are brought into the action, then the story line embraces their point of view as well, but the action always returns to the main character. In a novel the action takes place inside the character's head, within the *mindscape* of dramatic action.

In a play, the action, or story line, occurs onstage, under the proscenium arch, and the audience becomes the fourth wall, eavesdropping on the lives of the characters. They talk about their hopes and dreams, past and future plans, discuss their needs and desires, fears and conflicts. In this case, the action of the play occurs within the *language* of dramatic action; it is spoken, in *words*.

Movies are different. Film is a visual medium that dramatizes a basic story line; it deals in pictures, images, bits and pieces of film: a clock ticking, a window opening, someone watching, two people laughing, a car pulling away from the curb, a phone ringing. A screenplay is a story told with pictures, in dialogue and description, and placed within the context of dramatic structure.

A screenplay is like a noun—it's about a *person,* or persons, in a *place* or places, doing his or her or their *"thing."* All screenplays execute this basic premise. The person is the character, and doing his or her thing is the action.

If a screenplay is a story told with pictures, what then do all stories have in common? A beginning, a middle and an end, though not always in that order. If we were to take a screenplay and hang it on a wall like a painting and look at it, it would look like the diagram on page 9.

This basic linear structure is the *form* of the screenplay; it holds all the elements of the story line in place.

To understand the dynamics of structure, it's important to start with the word itself. The root of structure, *struct,* means "to build" or "to put something together" like a building or a car. But there is another definition of the word structure, and that is "the relationship between the parts and the whole."

The parts and the whole. Chess, for example, is a *whole* composed of four parts: the pieces—queen, king, bishop, pawns, knights, etc.; *the player or players,* because someone has to play the game of chess; *the board,* because you can't play chess without it; and the last thing you need to play chess is the *rules,* because they make chess the game it is. Those four things—pieces, player or players, board, and rules, the parts—are integrated into a whole, and the result is the game of chess. It is the relationship between the parts and the whole that determines the game.

A story is a whole, and the parts that make it—the action, characters, scenes, sequences, Acts I, II, III, incidents, episodes, events, music, locations, etc.—are what make up the story. It is a whole.

Structure is what holds the story in place. It is the relationship between these parts that holds the entire screenplay, the whole, together.

It is the paradigm of dramatic structure.

A paradigm is a model, example, or conceptual scheme.

The paradigm of a table, for example, is a top with four legs. Within that paradigm, we can have a low table, a high table, a narrow table, a wide table; or a circular table, a square table, a rectangular table; or a glass table, a wood table, a plastic table, wrought iron table, whatever, and the paradigm doesn't change—it remains firm, a top with four legs.

If a screenplay were a painting hanging on the wall, this is what it would look like:

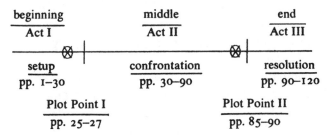

This is the paradigm of a screenplay.
Here's how it's broken down.

ACT I, or THE SETUP

Aristotle talks about the three unities of dramatic action: time, place, and action. The normal Hollywood film is approximately two hours long, or 120 minutes, while the European, or foreign film, is approximately 90 minutes. The way it works is that a page of screenplay equals approximately a minute of screen time. It doesn't matter whether the script is all action, all dialogue, or any combination of the two; generally speaking, a page of screenplay equals a minute of screen time.

Act I, the beginning, is a unit of dramatic action that is approximately thirty pages long and is held together with the dramatic context known as the *setup*. Context is the space that holds the content of the story in place. (The space inside a glass, for example, is a context; it "holds" the content in place—water, beer, milk, coffee, tea, juice; the space inside a glass can even hold raisins, trail mix, nuts, grapes, etc.)

The screenwriter has approximately thirty pages to *set up* the story, the characters, the dramatic premise, the situation (the circumstances surrounding the action) and to establish the relationships between the main character and the other people who inhabit the landscape of his or her world. When you go to a movie, you can usually determine—consciously or unconsciously—whether you "like" the movie or "do not like" the movie within the first ten minutes. The next time you go to a movie, find out how long it takes you to make that decision.

Ten minutes is ten pages of screenplay. This first ten-page unit of dramatic action is the most important part of the screenplay because you have to show the reader who your main character is, what the dramatic premise of the story (what it's about) is, and what the dramatic situation (the circumstances surrounding the action) is. In *Chinatown,* for example, we learn on the first page that Jake Gittes (Jack Nicholson), the main character, is a sleazy private detective specializing in "discreet investigation." And he has a certain flair for it. On page 5 we are introduced to a certain Mrs. Mulwray (Diane Ladd), who wants to hire Jake Gittes to find out "who my husband is having an affair with." That is the dramatic premise of the film, because the answer to that question is what leads us into the story. The dramatic premise is what the screenplay is about; it provides the dramatic thrust that drives the story to its conclusion.

In *Witness* (Earl Wallace and William Kelley), the first ten pages reveal the world of the Amish in Lancaster County, Pennsylvania, and the death of Rachel's husband takes her and her young child to Philadelphia, where the boy happens to witness the murder of an undercover cop, and that leads to the relationship with the main character, John Book, played by Harrison Ford. The entire first act is designed to reveal the dramatic premise and situation, and the relationship between an Amish woman and a tough Philadelphia cop.

ACT II, or THE CONFRONTATION

Act II is a unit of dramatic action that is approximately sixty pages long, goes from page 30 to page 90, and is held together with the dramatic context known as confrontation. During the second act the main character encounters obstacle after obstacle after obstacle that keeps him from achieving his or her dramatic need. Just look at *The Fugitive*. The entire story is driven by the main character's dramatic need to bring his wife's killer to justice. Dramatic need is defined as what your main character wants to win, gain, get, or achieve during the screenplay. What drives him or her forward through the action? What does your main character want? What is his or her need? If you know the character's dramatic need, you can create obstacles to that need, and the story becomes the main character overcoming obstacle after obstacle after obstacle to achieve (or not achieve) his or her dramatic need.

In *Chinatown,* a detective story, Act II deals with Jack Nicholson colliding with people who try to keep him from finding out who's responsible for the murder of Hollis Mulwray, and who's behind the water scandal. The obstacles that Jake Gittes encounters and overcomes dictate the dramatic action of the story.

All drama is conflict. Without conflict you have no character; without character, you have no action; without action, you have no story; and without story, you have no screenplay.

ACT III, or THE RESOLUTION

Act III is a unit of dramatic action that goes from the end of Act II, approximately page 90, to the end of the screenplay, and is held together with the dramatic context known as resolution. Resolution does not mean ending; resolution means solution. What is the solution of the screenplay? Does your main character live or die? Succeed or fail? Marry the man or woman, or not? Win the race or not? Win the election or not? Leave her husband or not? Act III *resolves* the story; it is not the ending. The ending is that specific scene, shot, or sequence that ends the script; it is not the solution of the story.

Beginning, middle, and end; Act I, Act II, and Act III. Setup, confrontation, resolution—the parts that make up the whole.

But this brings up another question: If these are some of the parts that make up the screenplay, how do you get from Act I, the setup, into Act II, the confrontation? And how do you get from Act II into Act III, the resolution? The answer is simple: Create a plot point at the end of Act I and Act II.

A plot point is any incident, episode, or event that "hooks" into the action and spins it around into another direction—in this case, Act II and Act III. A plot point occurs at the end of Act I, at about pages 20 to 25. It is a function of the main character. In *Chinatown*, after the newspaper story is released claiming Mr. Mulwray has been caught in a "love nest," the *real* Mrs. Mulwray (Faye Dunaway) arrives with her attorney and threatens to sue Jake Gittes and have his license revoked. (This is the dramatic situation; without his detective license, he can't function.) But if she is the real Mrs. Mulwray, who was the woman who hired Jake Gittes? And *why*? And who hired the phony Mrs. Mulwray? And *why*? The arrival of the real Mrs. Mulwray is what "hooks" into the action and spins it around into Act II. Jake Gittes must find out who set him up, and why. It happens at about page 23.

In *Witness,* after John Book has gone through all the lineups and mug shots trying to identify the killer, he is talking on the phone, and we follow Samuel, the young boy, as he wanders around the police station. He stops at the trophy case and examines the trophies lined up inside, and catches sight of a newspaper story pinned up inside. He looks closer at the picture in the article and identifies the man pictured as the killer of the undercover cop on page 10 of the screenplay. Book sees him, puts down the phone's receiver, and walks to the boy in slow motion, then kneels down beside him. Samuel points at the picture, and Book nods his head in understanding. He knows who the murderer is. Now he has to bring him to justice. It is Plot Point I. It occurs on page 25 of the screenplay.

The plot point at the end of the second act is also an incident, episode, or event that "hooks" into the action, and spins it around into Act III. It usually occurs at about page 85 or 90 of the screenplay. In *Chinatown*, Plot Point II is when Jack Nicholson finds a pair of horn-rim glasses in the pond where Hollis Mulwray was murdered, and knows they belong to Mulwray, or to the person who killed him. This leads to the resolution of the story.

In *Witness,* after Book learns that his partner has been killed, he knows it's time to go back to Philadelphia and bring the guilty policemen to justice. But before he can leave, he must complete his relationship with Rachel.

When Rachel (Kelly McGillis) learns that Book is leaving, she carefully puts her hat on the floor, then runs to him, and they kiss and embrace and at last give in to their real feelings. This incident completes the action of Act II and sets the stage for Act III, when the killers appear to kill Book before he can tell anyone. The entire action of Act III deals with the shoot-out between Book and the three policemen. It is the resolution of the screenplay. The ending is when Book drives down the dirt road and the final end credits come up.

Do all good screenplays fit the paradigm? Yes. But that doesn't make them good screenplays, or good movies. The paradigm is a form, not a formula. Form is what holds something together; it's structure, it's configuration. The form of a coat or jacket, for example, is two arms, a front and a back. And within that form of two arms, front and back, you can have any variation of style, fabric, and color, but the form remains intact.

A formula, however, is totally different. In a formula, certain elements are put together so they come out *exactly the same* every time. If you put that coat on an assembly line, every coat will be exactly the same, with the same pattern, the same fabric, the same color, the same cut, the same material. It will not change, except for size.

The paradigm is a form, not a formula; it's what holds the story together. The spine, the skeleton, and the story are what determine structure; structure doesn't determine story.

Dramatic structure of the screenplay may be defined as a

linear arrangement of related incidents, episodes, or events leading to a dramatic resolution. How you utilize these structural components determines the form of your film. *Annie Hall,* for example, is a story told in flashback, but it has a definite beginning, middle, and end. *Last Year at Marienbad* does, too, though not in that order. So do *Citizen Kane; Hiroshima, Mon Amour; Dances With Wolves; The Silence of the Lambs,* and *The Fugitive.*

There is only form, not formula. The paradigm is a model, an example, or conceptual scheme; it is what a well-structured screenplay looks like, an overview of the story line as it unfolds from beginning to end.

Do all good screenplays fit the paradigm?

Screenplays that work follow the paradigm. But don't take my word for it. Go to any movie and see whether you can determine its structure.

Some of you may not believe that. You may not believe in beginnings, middles, and ends, either. You may say that art, like life, is nothing more than several individual "moments" suspended in some giant middle, with no beginning and no end, what Kurt Vonnegut calls "a series of random moments" strung together in a haphazard fashion.

I disagree.

Birth? Life? Death? Isn't that a beginning, middle, and end?

Think about the rise and fall of great civilizations—of Egypt, Greece, the Roman Empire, rising from the seed of a small community to the apex of power, then disintegrating and dying.

Think about the birth and death of a star, or the beginning of the Universe, according to the "Big Bang" theory that most scientists now agree on. If there's a beginning to the Universe, is there going to be an end?

Think about the cells in our bodies. How often are they

replenished, restored, and recreated? Every seven years—within a seven-year cycle, the cells in our bodies are born, function, die, and are reborn again.

Think about the first day of a new job, meeting new people, assuming new responsibilities; you stay there until you decide to leave, retire, or are fired.

Screenplays are no different. They have a definite beginning, middle, and end.

It is the *foundation of dramatic structure.*

If you don't believe the *paradigm,* check it out. Prove me wrong. Go to a movie—go see several movies—see whether it fits the *paradigm* or not.

If you're interested in writing screenplays, you should be doing this all the time. Every movie you see then becomes a learning process, expanding your awareness and comprehension of what a movie is, or is not.

You should also read as many screenplays as possible in order to expand your awareness of the form and structure. Many screenplays have been reprinted in book form and most bookstores have them, or can order them. Several are already out of print, but you can check your library or local university theater arts library to see whether or not they have screenplays available.

I have my students read and study scripts like *Chinatown, Network, Rocky, Three Days of the Condor, The Hustler* (in paperback, *Three Screenplays* by Robert Rossen, now out of print), *Annie Hall,* and *Harold and Maude.* These scripts are excellent teaching aids. If they aren't available, read any screenplay you can find. The more the better.

The *paradigm* works.

It is the *foundation* of a good screenplay.

∗   ∗   ∗

As an exercise: Go to a movie. After the lights dim and the credits begin, ask yourself how long it takes you to make a decision about whether you "like" or "dis-like" the movie. Be aware of your decision, then look at your watch.

If you find a movie you really enjoy, go back and see it again. See if the movie falls into the *paradigm*. See if you can determine the breakdown of each act. Find the beginning, middle, and end. Note how the story is set up, how long it takes you to find out what is going on in the movie, and whether or not you're hooked into the film, or dragged into it. Find the plot points at the end of Act I, and Act II, and how they lead to the resolution.

2

The Subject

Wherein we explore the nature of the subject:

What is the SUBJECT of your screenplay?

What is it about?

Remember that a screenplay is like a noun—a person in a place, doing his/her "thing." The person is the *main character* and doing his/her "thing" is the *action*. When we talk about the subject of a screenplay, we're talking about *action* and *character*.

Action is *what happens*; character, *who* it happens to. Every screenplay dramatizes action and character. You must know who your movie is about and what happens to him or her. It is a primary concept in writing.

If you have an idea about three guys holding up the Chase Manhattan Bank, you've got to express it dramatically. And that means focusing on your *characters*, the three guys, and the *action*, holding up the Chase Manhattan Bank.

Every screenplay has a subject. *Bonnie and Clyde*, for example, is a story about the Clyde Barrow Gang holding up banks in the Midwest during the Depression, and their eventual downfall. Action and character. It is essential to isolate your generalized idea into a specific dramatic premise. And that becomes the starting point of your screenplay.

Every story has a definite beginning, middle, and end. In *Bonnie and Clyde*, the beginning dramatizes the meetings of Bonnie and Clyde and the forming of their gang. In the middle they hold up several banks and the law goes after them. In the end, they are caught by the forces of society and killed. Setup, confrontation, and resolution.

When you can articulate your subject in a few sentences, in terms of action and character, you begin expanding the elements of form and structure. It may take several pages of writing about your story before you can begin to grasp the essentials and reduce a complex story into a simple sentence or two. Don't worry about it. Just keep doing it, and you will be able to articulate your story idea clearly and concisely.

That is your responsibility. If you don't know what your story is about, who does? The reader? The viewer? If you don't know what you're writing about, how do you expect someone else to know? The writer always exercises *choice* and *responsibility* in determining the dramatic execution of the story. Choice and responsibility—these words will be a familiar refrain throughout this book. Every creative decision must be made by *choice*, not necessity. If your character *walks* out of a bank, that's one story. If he *runs* out of a bank, that's another story.

Many people already have ideas they want to write into a screenplay. Others don't. How do you go about finding a subject?

An idea in a newspaper, or on the TV news, or an incident that might have happened to a friend or relative can be the subject of a movie. *Dog Day Afternoon* was a newspaper article before it became a movie. When you're looking for a subject, your subject is looking for you. You'll find it someplace, at some time, probably when you're least expecting it. It will be yours to do or not do, as you choose. *Chinatown* grew out of a Los Angeles water scandal found in an old newspaper of that period. *Shampoo* grew out of several incidents that happened to a celebrated Hollywood hair stylist. *Taxi Driver* is a story about the loneliness of driving a cab in New York City. *Bonnie and Clyde, Butch Cassidy and the Sundance Kid, All the President's Men,* grew out of real people in real situations. Your subject will find you. Just give yourself the opportunity to find it. It's very simple. Trust yourself. Just start looking for an action and a character.

When you can express your idea succinctly in terms of action and character, when you can express it like a noun—my story is about this person, in this place, doing his/her "thing"—you're beginning the preparation of your screenplay.

The next step is expanding your subject. Fleshing out the action and focusing on the character broadens the story line and accentuates the details. Gather your material any way you can. It will always be to your advantage.

A lot of people wonder about the value, or necessity, of doing research. As far as I'm concerned, research is absolutely essential. All writing entails research, and research means gathering information. Remember, the hardest part of writing is knowing what to write.

By doing research—whether in written sources such as books, magazines, or newspapers or through personal interviews—you acquire information. The information you collect allows you to operate from the position of choice and responsibility. You can either choose to use some, or all, or none of the material you've gathered; that's your choice, dictated by the terms of the story. Not using it because you don't have it offers you no choice at all, and will always work against you and your story.

Too many people start writing with only a vague, half-formed idea in their heads. It works for about 30 pages, then falls apart. You don't know what to do next, or where to go, and you get angry and confused and frustrated, and just give up.

If it is necessary or possible to conduct personal interviews, you'll be surprised to find that most people are willing to help you any way they can, and they'll often go out of their way to assist you in your search for accurate information. Personal interviews have another advantage: They can give you a more immediate and spontaneous slant than any book, newspaper, or magazine story. It's the next best thing to having experienced something yourself. Remember: The more you know, the more you can communicate. And be in a position of choice and responsibility when making creative decisions.

I recently had the opportunity of working on a story with Craig Breedlove, onetime holder of the World Land Speed Record, and the first man to go 400, 500, and 600 miles per hour on land. Craig created a rocket car that traveled at a speed of 400 miles per hour for a quarter mile. The rocket system was the same system used to land a man on the moon.

The story is about a man breaking the World Water Speed Record in a rocket boat. But a rocket boat doesn't exist, at least not yet. I had to do all kinds of research to find out about my subject matter. What is the Water Speed Record? Where do you go to break the record? Is it possible for a rocket boat to beat the record? How do the officials time the boats? Is a speed of over 400 miles per hour on water possible? Out of our conversations I learned about rocket systems, the Water Speed Record, and designing and building a racing boat. And out of those conversations came an action and a character. And a way to fuse fact and fiction into a dramatic story line.

The rule bears repetition: The more you know, the more you can communicate.

Research is essential in writing the screenplay. Once you choose a subject, and can state it briefly in a sentence or two, you can begin preliminary research. Determine where you can go to increase your knowledge of the subject. Paul Schrader, who wrote *Taxi Driver*, wanted to write a movie that took place on a train. So he took a train from Los Angeles to New York, and when he stepped off the train he realized he didn't have a story. He hadn't found one. That's okay. Choose another subject. Schrader went on to write *Obsession*, and Colin Higgins, who wrote *Harold and Maude*, went on to write the train story, *Silver Streak*. Richard Brooks spent eight months researching *Bite the Bullet* before he put one word on paper. He did the same thing with *The Professionals* and *In Cold Blood*, even though the latter was based on a very well researched book by Truman Capote. Waldo Salt, who wrote *Midnight Cowboy*, worked on a screenplay for Jane Fonda, entitled *Coming Home*. His research included speaking to more than 26 paralyzed Vietnam veterans, which resulted in some 200 hours of taped interviews.

If you're writing a story about a bicycle racer, for example, what kind of racer is he? A sprinter or a long-distance racer? Where do bicycle races take place? Where do you want to set your story? In what city? Are there different types of races, or racing circuits? Associations and clubs? How many races are held throughout the year? What about international competition? Does it affect your story? The character? What kind of bikes do they use? How do you become a bicycle racer? These questions must be answered before you start putting words on paper.

Research gives you ideas, a sense of people, situation, and locale. It allows you to gain a degree of confidence so you are always on top of your subject, operating from choice, not necessity or ignorance.

Start with your subject. When you think subject, think action and character. If we draw a diagram, it looks like this:

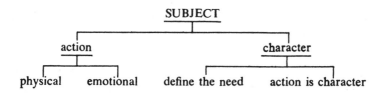

There are two kinds of action—*physical* action and *emotional* action. Physical action is holding up a bank, as in *Dog Day Afternoon*; a car chase, as in *Bullitt* or *The French Connection*; a race, or competition, or game, as in *Rollerball*. Emotional action is what happens inside your characters during the story. Emotional action is the center of the drama in *Love Story, Alice Doesn't Live Here Anymore*, and *La Notte*, Antonioni's masterpiece about a disintegrating marriage. Most films contain both kinds of action.

Chinatown creates a delicate balance of physical and emotional action. What happens to Jack Nicholson when he uncovers the water scandal is related to his own feelings about Faye Dunaway.

In *Taxi Driver* Paul Schrader wanted to dramatize the experience of loneliness. So he chose as his image a cabdriver. A cab, like a ship at sea, goes from port to port, fare to fare. The cabbie in his screenplay, as dramatic metaphor, cruises around the city with no emotional ties, no roots, no connection, a lonely, solitary existence.

Ask yourself what kind of story you are writing. Is it an outdoor action-adventure movie, or is it a story about a relationship, an emotional story? Once you determine what kind of action you're dealing with, you can move into your character.

First, *define the need* of your character. What does your character want? What is his need? What drives him to the resolution of your story? In *Chinatown* Jack Nicholson's need is finding out *who* set him up, and *why*. In *Three Days of the Condor*, Robert Redford needs to know *who* wants to kill him, and *why*. You must define the need of your character. What does he want?

Al Pacino holds up the bank in *Dog Day Afternoon* to get money for a sex-change operation for his male lover. That is his need. If your character creates a system to beat the tables in Las Vegas, how much does he need to win before he knows if the system works or doesn't? The need of your character gives you a goal, a destination, an ending to your story. How your character achieves or does not achieve that goal becomes the action of your story.

All drama is conflict. If you know the *need* of your character, you can create obstacles to fulfill that need. How he overcomes those obstacles is your story. Conflict, struggle, overcoming obstacles, are the primary ingredients in all drama. In comedy, too. It is the writer's responsibility to generate enough conflict to keep the audience, or reader, interested. The story always has to move forward, toward its resolution.

And it all comes down to knowing your subject. If you know the action and character of your screenplay, you can define the need of your character and then create obstacles to realizing that need.

The dramatic need of three guys holding up the Chase Manhattan Bank is directly related to the action of holding up the bank. The obstacles to that need create the conflict—the various alarm systems, the vault, the locks, the security measures that must be overcome for them to get away. (No one robs a bank to get caught!) The characters must plan what they do, and that means extensive observation and research, and preparing a well-coordinated plan of action before they can even attempt the robbery. The days of Bonnie and Clyde simply "dropping by" and robbing a bank are over.

In *Midnight Cowboy*, Jon Voight comes to New York to hustle women. That is his need. It is also his dream. And, as far as he's concerned, he's going to make a lot of money and satisfy a lot of women in the process.

What are the obstacles he immediately confronts? He gets hustled by Dustin Hoffman, loses his money, doesn't have any friends or a job, and the women of New York don't even acknowledge his existence. Some dream! His need collides head-on with the harsh reality of New York City. That's conflict!

Without conflict there is no drama. Without need, there is no character. Without character, there is no action. "Action is Character," F. Scott Fitzgerald wrote in *The Last Tycoon*. What a person *does* is what he *is*, not what he says!

When you begin to explore your subject, you will see that all things are related in your screenplay. Nothing is thrown in by chance, or just because it's cute or clever. "There's a special Providence in the fall of a sparrow," Shakespeare observed. "For every action there is an equal and opposite reaction" is a natural law of the Universe. The same principle applies to your story. It is the subject of your screenplay. KNOW YOUR SUBJECT!

*   *   *

As an exercise: Find a subject you want to treat in screenplay form. Reduce it to a few sentences in terms of action and character, and write it out.

3

Character

Wherein we discuss the creation of character:

How do you go about creating character?

What is character? How do you determine whether your character will drive a car, or ride a bicycle? How do you establish a relationship between your character, his action, and the story you're telling?

Character is the essential foundation of your screenplay. It is the heart and soul and nervous system of your story. Before you put a word on paper, you must know your character.

KNOW YOUR CHARACTER.

Who is your main character? Who is your story about? If your story is about three guys holding up the Chase Manhattan Bank, which one of the three characters is the *main character*? You must select one person as the main character.

Who is the main character in *Butch Cassidy and the Sundance Kid*? Butch is. He is the man making the decisions. Butch has a great line where he broaches one of his usual wild schemes to Sundance, and Robert Redford just looks at Paul Newman, doesn't say a word, and turns away. And Newman mutters to himself: "I got vision and the rest of the world wears bifocals." And, it's true. Within the context of that screenplay, Butch Cassidy *is* the main character—he is the character who *plans* things, who *acts*. Butch leads and Sundance follows. It is Butch's idea to leave for South America; he knows their outlaw days are numbered, and to escape the law, death, or both, they must leave. He convinces Sundance and Etta Place to go with him. Sundance is a *major* character, not the *main* character. Once you establish the main character, you can explore ways to create a full-bodied, dimensional character portrait.

There are several ways to approach characterization, all valid, but you must choose the best way for you. The method outlined below will give you the opportunity to choose what you want to use, or not use, in developing your characters.

First, establish your main character. Then separate the components of his/her life into two basic categories: *interior* and *exterior*. The interior life of your character takes place from birth until the moment your film begins. It is a process that *forms* character. The exterior life of your character takes place from the moment your film begins to the conclusion of the story. It is a process that *reveals* character.

Film is a visual medium. You must find ways to reveal your character's conflicts *visually*. You cannot reveal what you don't know.

Thus, the distinction between *knowing* your character and revealing him or her on paper.

Diagrammed, it looks like this:

CHARACTER

(*from birth till present*)	(*from start of movie to end*)
INTERIOR	.... EXTERIOR
FORMS | CHARACTER	REVEALS |CHARACTER
⌐character⌐	⌐ define action is ⌐
biography	the need character

Start with the *interior* life. Is your character male or female? If male, how old is he when the story begins? Where does he live? What city or country? Then—where was he born? Was he an only child, or did he have any brothers or sisters? What kind of childhood did he have? Happy? Sad? What was his relationship to his parents? What kind of child was he? Outgoing, an extrovert; or studious, an introvert?

When you start formulating your character from birth, you see your character build in body and form. Pursue this through his school years, then into college. Is he married, single, widowed, separated, or divorced? If married, for how long and to whom? Childhood sweetheart; blind date; long courtship or none?

Writing is the ability to ask yourself questions and get the answers. That's why I call developing your character creative research. You're asking questions and getting answers.

Once you've established the interior aspect of your character in a character biography, move into the *exterior* portion of your story.

The *exterior* aspect of your character takes place from the moment your screenplay begins to the final fade-out. It is important to examine the relationships within the lives of your characters.

Who are they and what do they do? Are they sad or happy with their life, or life-style? Do they wish their lives were different, with another job, or another wife, or possibly wish they were someone else?

How do you reveal your characters on paper?

First, isolate the elements or components of their life. You must create your people in relationship to other people, or things. All dramatic characters interact in three ways:

1) *They experience conflict in achieving their dramatic need.*
They need money, for example, to buy the necessary

equipment to rob the Chase Manhattan Bank. How do they get it? Steal it? Rob a person, or store?

2) *They interact with other characters,* either in an antagonistic, friendly, or indifferent way. Drama is conflict, remember. Jean Renoir, the famous French film director, once told me it's more effective dramatically to portray a son of a bitch than a nice guy. It's worth thinking about.

3) *They interact with themselves.* Our main character might have to overcome his fear of prison to pull off the robbery successfully. Fear is an emotional element that must be confronted and defined in order to be overcome. All of us who have been "victims" at one time or another know that.

How do you make your characters real, multidimensional people?

First, separate your character's life into three basic components—*professional, personal,* and *private.*

Professional: What does your character do for a living? Where does he work? Is he the vice-president of a bank? A construction worker? A bum? A scientist? A pimp? What does he or she do?

If your character works in an office, what does he do in the office? What is his relationship with his coworkers? Do they get along? Help each other? Confide in each other? Socialize with each other during off-hours? How does he get along with his boss? Is it a good relationship, or is there some resentment because of the way things are going, or inadequate salary? When you can define and explore the relationships of your main character to the other people in his life, you're creating a personality and a point of view. And that is the starting point of characterization.

Personal: Is your main character single, widowed, married, separated, or divorced? If married, whom did he marry? When? What is their relationship like? Social or isolated? Many friends and social functions, or few friends? Is the marriage solid, or is your character thinking about, or participating in, extramarital affairs? If single, what is his single life like? Is he divorced? There are a lot of dramatic possibilities in a divorced person. When you have doubts about your character, go into your own life. Ask yourself—if you were in that situation, what would you do in your character's place? Define the personal relationships of your character.

Private: What does your character do when he or she is by himself? Watch TV? Exercise—jogging or bicycling, for example? Does he have any pets? What kind? Does he collect stamps or participate in some interesting hobbies? In short, this covers the area of your character's life when he or she is alone.

What is the *need* of your character? What does he or she want in your screenplay? *Define the need of your character.* If your story is about a racecar driver racing in the Indianapolis 500, he wants to win the race. That is his need. Warren Beatty's need in *Shampoo* is to open up his own shop. That need propels him through the action of the screenplay. In *Rocky*, Rocky's need is to be on his feet at the end of 15 rounds with Apollo Creed.

Once you define the need of your character, you can create obstacles to that need. Drama is conflict. You must be clear on your character's need so you can create obstacles to that need. This gives your story a *dramatic tension* often missing from a novice's screenplay.

If we diagram the concept of character, it would look like the example on the page opposite.

The essence of character is *action*. Your character is what he does. Film is a visual medium, and the writer's responsibility is to choose an image, or picture, that cinematically

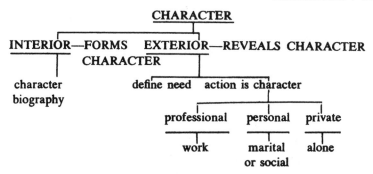

dramatizes his character. You can create a dialogue scene in a small and stuffy hotel room, or have the scene occur at the beach. One is visually closed; the other is visually open and dynamic. It's your story, your choice.

A screenplay, remember, is a story told with pictures. And "every picture tells a story," sings Rod Stewart. Pictures, or images, reveal aspects of character. In Robert Rossen's classic film *The Hustler*, a physical defect symbolizes an aspect of character. The girl played by Piper Laurie is a cripple; she walks with a limp. She is also an emotional cripple; she drinks too much, has no sense of aim or purpose in life. The physical limp underscores her emotional qualities—*visually*.

Sam Peckinpah does this in *The Wild Bunch*. The character played by William Holden walks with a limp, the result of an aborted holdup some years before. It represents an aspect of Holden's character, revealing him to be an "unchanged man in a changing land," one of Peckinpah's favorite themes; a man born ten years too late, a man out of time. In *Chinatown*, Nicholson gets his nose slit because, as a detective, he's "nosy."

Physical handicap—as an aspect of characterization—is a theatrical convention that extends far back into the past. One thinks of *Richard III*, or the use of consumption or VD that strike the characters in the dramas of O'Neill and Ibsen, respectively.

Form your characters by creating a character biography, then reveal them by their actions, and possible physical traits. ACTION IS CHARACTER.

What about dialogue?

DIALOGUE is a function of character. If you know your character, your dialogue should flow easily in line with the unfolding of your story. But many people worry about their dialogue; it might be awkward and stilted. It probably is. So what? Writing dialogue is a learning process, an act of co-ordination. It gets easier the more you do. It's okay for the first 60 pages of your first draft to be filled with awkward dialogue. Don't worry about it. The last 60 pages will be smooth and functional. The more you do it, the easier it gets. Then you can go back and smooth out the dialogue in the first part of the screenplay.

What is the function of dialogue?

Dialogue is related to your character's need, his hopes and dreams.

What should dialogue do?

Dialogue must communicate information or the facts of your story to the audience. It must move the story forward. It must reveal character. Dialogue must reveal conflicts between and within characters, and emotional states and personality quirks of character; dialogue comes out of character.

KNOW YOUR CHARACTER!

*   *   *

As an exercise: Take your subject idea of action and character. Choose your main character and select two or three major characters. Write character biographies of three to ten pages, or longer if necessary. Start from birth and carry it into the present, until the story starts. This applies to past lives as well, if you like.

Isolate the three P's to create your main character's relationships during the screenplay. Think about your people.

4

Building a Character

*Wherein we expand on the process
of building character:*

We've touched upon the foundations of character creation through the character biography and isolating his relationships.

Now what?

How do you take the *idea* of a person, as it exists in scrambled, fragmented form, and make him or her into a living, flesh-and-blood person? A person you can relate to and identify with?

How do you go about "putting life" into your characters? How do you build character?

It's a question that poets, philosophers, writers, artists, scientists, and the Church have pondered since the beginning of recorded time. There is no definite answer—it's part and parcel of the mystery and magic of the creative process.

The key word is "process." There is a way to do it.

First, create the *context* of character. Then fill the context with *content*. *Context* and *content*. These are abstract principles that offer you an invaluable tool in the creative process. They comprise a concept that will be used often in the book.

This is *context*:

Imagine an empty coffee cup. Look inside it. There is a space inside that cup. The *space* inside *holds* the coffee, tea, milk, water, hot chocolate, beer, or whatever liquid is the *content* of that cup.

The cup *holds* the coffee. The space inside the cup that holds the coffee is *context*.

Hold that image and the concept will become clear as we progress.

Let's explore the process of building a character in terms of context.

First—define the NEED of your character.

What does your character want to achieve, or get, during the course of your screenplay?

Is it a million dollars? To rob the Chase Manhattan Bank? To break the Water Speed Record? To go to New York and become a "midnight cowboy," like Jon Voight? To sustain the relationship with "Annie Hall"? To realize a life-long dream to become a singer in Monterey, California, like Alice in *Alice Doesn't Live Here Anymore*? To find out "what's going on?" like Richard Dreyfuss in *Close Encounters of the Third Kind*? These are all character needs.

Ask yourself—what is the NEED of your character?

Then, do the character biography. As suggested, write anywhere from three to ten pages, or more if you like. Find out who your character is. You may want to start with your character's grandparents to obtain a clear picture for yourself. Don't worry about how many pages you write. You are beginning a process that will continue to grow and expand during the creative preparation of your screenplay. The biography is for you and does not have to be included in the screenplay at all. It is only a tool for you to use in creating your character.

When your character biography is completed, move into the *exterior* portion of your characters. Isolate the *professional, personal,* and *private* elements of your character's life.

That's the start point. *Context.*

Now, let's explore the question WHAT IS CHARACTER?

What *is* character?

What do all people have in common? We're the same, you and I; we have the same needs, the same wants, the same fears and insecurities; we want to be loved, to have people like us, to succeed, be happy and healthy. We're all the same under the skin. Certain things unite us.

What separates us?

What separates us from everyone else is our POINT OF VIEW—how we view the world. Every person has a point of view.

CHARACTER IS A POINT OF VIEW—it is the way we look at the world. It is a *context.*

Your character could be a parent, and thus represent a "parent's" point of view. He or she could be a student, and would view the world from a "student's" point of view. Your character could be a political activist, like Vanessa Redgrave in *Julia.* That is her point of view, and she gives her life for it. A housewife has a specific point of view. A criminal, a terrorist, a cop, a doctor, lawyer, rich man, poor man, a woman, liberated or otherwise—all present individual and specific *points of view.*

What is your character's point of view?

Is your character liberal or conservative? Is he or she an environmentalist? A humanist? A racist? Someone who believes in fate, destiny, or astrology? Someone who puts their faith in doctors, lawyers, the *Wall Street Journal,* and *The*

New York Times? A believer in *Time, People,* and *Newsweek?*

What is your character's point of view about his work? About his marriage? Does your character like music? If so, what kind? These elements become specific and integral parts of your character.

We all have a point of view—make sure your characters have specific and individual points of view. Create the *context,* and the *content* follows.

For example, your character's point of view may be that the indiscriminate killing of whales and dolphins is morally wrong, and he supports that point of view by giving donations, volunteering his services, attending meetings, participating in demonstrations, wearing a T-shirt with SAVE THE WHALES AND DOLPHINS on it. Dolphins and whales are two of the most intelligent species on the planet. Some scientists speculate they may be "smarter than man." Scientific data supports the fact that the dolphin has never hurt or attacked a member of the human species. There are numerous tales of dolphins protecting downed World War II flyers and navymen against the vicious onslaught of sharks. There must be a way to save these intelligent life-forms. Your character, for example, may boycott tuna as a means of protesting the senseless slaughter of whales and dolphins by commercial fishermen.

Look for ways your characters can support and dramatize their points of view.

What else is character?

Character is also an ATTITUDE—a *context*—a way of acting or feeling that reveals a person's opinion. Is your character superior in attitude? Inferior? A positive person, or negative? Optimistic or pessimistic? Enthusiastic about life or job, or unhappy?

Drama is conflict, remember—the more clearly you can define your character's need, the easier it becomes to create obstacles to that need, thus generating conflict. This supports you in creating a tense, dramatic story line.

It's an effective rule in comedy as well. Neil Simon's characters usually have a simple need that sparks conflict. In *The Goodbye Girl*, Richard Dreyfuss plays an actor from Chicago who sublets a New York apartment from a friend, and when he arrives he finds the apartment "occupied" by his friend's former roommate (Marsha Mason) and her young daughter (Quinn Cummings). He wants in, and she won't leave—the apartment is hers, she claims, and possession *is* nine-tenths of the law. This conflict is the beginning of their relationship, based on the attitude that each is "right."

Adam's Rib is another case in point. Written by Garson Kanin and Ruth Gordon, it stars Spencer Tracy and Katharine Hepburn as two attorneys—husband and wife—pitted against each other in the courtroom. Tracy is prosecuting a woman (Judy Holliday) charged with shooting her husband, and Hepburn is defending her! It is a magnificent comedic situation dealing with basic questions of "equal rights" for men and women. Made in 1949, it anticipated the struggle for women's rights, and remains a classic American film comedy.

Define your character's need, then create obstacles to that need.

The more you know about your character the easier it is to create dimension within the fabric of your story.

What else is character?

Character is PERSONALITY. Every character visually manifests a personality. Is your character cheerful? Happy, bright, witty, or outgoing? Serious? Shy? Retiring? Charming in manner, or uncouth, sloppy, surly, without wit or humor?

What kind of personality does your character have?

Is she nonchalant, devilish, or mischievous? These are all personality traits—they all reflect character.

Character is also BEHAVIOR. The essence of character is action—what a person does is what he is.

Behavior is action. Suppose a character in a Rolls-Royce steps out of the car, locks it, then crosses the street. He sees a dime in the gutter—what does he do? If he looks around to see if anyone is watching, sees no one, then bends down and picks up the coin, that tells you something about his character. If he looks around, sees someone watching him, and *does not* pick up the dime, that, too, tells you something about his character, dramatized by his behavior.

If you establish your character's behavior within a dramatic situation, you may give the reader or audience insight into their own lives.

Behavior tells you a lot. A friend of mine had the opportunity of flying to New York for a business interview. She had mixed feelings about going. The interview was for a prestigious and high-salaried job she wanted; but she didn't know whether she was willing to move to New York. She wrestled with the problem for more than a week, then finally decided to go, packed her bags and drove to the airport. But when she parked her car at the airport, she "accidentally" locked her keys inside the car—with the motor running! It's a perfect example of a behavioral action revealing character; it told her what she knew all along—she didn't want to go to New York!

A scene like that illustrates a lot about character.

Does your character get angry easily, and react by throwing things as Marlon Brando did in *A Streetcar Named Desire*? Or, does he get intensely *angry*, like Marlon Brando in *The Godfather*, and smile grimly and not show it? Is your character late, or early, or on time for appointments? Does your character react to authority the way Woody Allen does in *Annie Hall* when he tears up his driver's license in front of a policeman? Every action and speech based on individual character traits expands our knowledge and comprehension of your characters.

If you reach a point in your screenplay where you don't know what your characters will do in a certain situation, go into your own life and find out what you would do in a similar situation. You're the best source material you have. Exercise it. If you created the problem, you can solve it.

It's the same in our everyday lives.

It all comes out of knowing your character. What does your character want to achieve during the course of the screenplay? What is it that drives him or her forward to achieve that goal? Or not achieve it? What is his need, or purpose, in your story? Why is he or she there? What do they want to get? What should we, the reader or audience, feel about your people? That's your job as writer—to create real people in real situations.

What else is character?

Character is also what I term REVELATION. During the story we learn something about your character. In *Three Days of the Condor*, for example, Robert Redford orders lunch at a neighborhood restaurant. We learn he is intelligent, a writer "with the finest collection of rejection slips in the world," and later we dramatically accept the way he adapts to his new situation—someone is out to kill him and he doesn't know *who* or *why*. Something is revealed to us about the character of Robert Redford in the tightly written screenplay by Lorenzo Semple, Jr., and David Rayfiel.

The screenwriter's function is to reveal aspects of character to the reader and audience. We must learn something about your character. During the progression of your screenplay, your character usually learns something about his plight in terms of the story at the same time the audience does. In this way, character and audience share in the discovery of plot points that sustain the dramatic action. IDENTIFICATION is also an aspect of character. The recognition factor of "I *know* someone like that" is the greatest compliment a writer can receive. ACTION IS CHARACTER—what a person does is what he is, not what he says.

All the above-mentioned character traits—point of view, personality, attitude, and behavior—are related and will overlap each other during the process of building your character. This puts you in a position of choice; you can choose to use some, or all, of these character traits, or none of them. Knowing what they are, though, expands your command of the process of building a character.

It all springs from the character biography; out of your character's past comes a point of view, a personality, an attitude, behavior, a need and purpose.

When you are in the writing process you will find it will take you anywhere from 20 to 50 pages before your characters start talking to you, telling you what *they* want to *do* and *say*. Once you've made contact, and established a connection with your people, they'll take over. Let them do what they want to do. Trust your ability to exercise the choice of action and direction during the "words on paper" stage.

Sometimes your characters might alter the story line and you may not know whether to let them do it, or not. Let them do it. See what happens. The worst that can happen is you'll spend a few days realizing you made a mistake. It's important to make mistakes; out of accidents, and mistakes, springs creative spontaneity. If you've made a mistake, simply rewrite that section and it will all fall into place.

One of my students came to me and told me he was writing a drama, complete with unhappy or "tragic" ending. But at the beginning of the third act, his characters started acting "funny." Gag lines started coming out, and the resolution became funny, not serious. Every time he sat down to write, the humor just poured out; he couldn't stop it. He became frustrated, finally gave up in despair.

He came to me almost apologetic. In all honesty, he explained, he didn't know what to do. I suggested that he sit down and start writing. Let the words and dialogue come out as they wanted to. If it's funny, let it be funny. Just write and complete the third act. Then he could see what he had. If it was funny all the way through and he didn't like it, all he had to do was put it in a drawer somewhere and file it away, and then go back and write the third act the way he wanted to in the first place.

He did it, and it worked. He threw out the comedy version of the third act, then wrote it serious, the way he wanted to. The comedy was something he *had* to do, something he *had* to get out. It was his way of avoiding "completing" the screenplay. Many times, writers on the verge of completing a project will hold onto it and not finish it. What are you going to do after it's complete? Do you ever read a book and hate to finish it? We all do it. Just recognize it as a natural phenomenon, and don't worry about it.

If it ever happens to you, simply write the material the way it comes out. See what happens. Writing is always an adventure; you never really *know* what's going to come out. The worst that can happen if you make a mistake is that you spend a few days rewriting something that didn't work!

Just don't expect your characters to start talking to you from page 1. It doesn't work that way. If you've done your creative research and KNOW YOUR CHARACTER, you're going to experience some resistance before you break through and get in touch with your people.

The end result of all your work and research and preparation and thinking time will be characters who are real and alive and believable; real people in real situations. That's what we all aim for.

*   *   *

As an exercise: Go into your character biographies and establish a specific *point of view* for your main character and three major ones. Create an *attitude*, and think about some *behavioral* or *personality* traits that will reveal your characters. Think about *context* and *content*. You're going to run into them again.

5

Creating a Character

Wherein we create a character and
uncover a story:

There are two ways to approach a screenplay. One is to get
an idea, then create your characters to fit that idea. "Three
guys holding up the Chase Manhattan Bank" is an example
of this. You take the idea, then "pour" your characters into
it: a down-and-out fighter getting an opportunity to fight the
Heavyweight Champion of the World, as in *Rocky*; a man
holding up a bank to get money for a sex-change operation, as
in *Dog Day Afternoon*; a man setting out to break the Water
Speed Record, as in *The Run*.

You create the characters to fit the idea.

The other way to approach a screenplay is by creating a
character; out of that character will emerge a need, an action,
and a story. Alice, in *Alice Doesn't Live Here Anymore*, is
an example of this. Jane Fonda had an idea about a character in a situation, expressed it to her associates, and *Coming
Home* was created. *The Turning Point* by Arthur Laurents
emerged from the characters eventually played by Shirley
MacLaine and Anne Bancroft. Create a character and you'll
create a story.

One of my favorite screenwriting classes at Sherwood

Oaks Experimental College was "creating a character." We built a character, male or female, and created an idea for a screenplay. Everyone participated, throwing out ideas and suggestions, and gradually a character began forming and we started shaping a story. It took a couple of hours, and we usually ended up with a solid character and sometimes a pretty good idea for a movie.

We had a good time, and it began a process that managed to parallel the symmetrical chaos of the creative experience. Creating a character *is* a process, and until you've done it, and experienced it, you're more than likely to stumble around awkwardly like a blind man in a fog.

How do you go about creating a character? We started from scratch. I asked a series of questions and the class responded with answers. I took the answers and shaped them into a character. And, out of that character, a story emerged.

Sometimes it worked beautifully; we came up with an interesting character and a good dramatic premise for a movie. Other times it didn't work. But considering the time we had and circumstances of the class, we didn't do badly at all.

The following is an edited and abridged version of a class that worked well. The questions go from the general to the specific, from *context* to *content*. When you read it, you might want to substitute your own answers for the ones we selected and make the story your own.

"We're going to participate in an exercise and create a character," I explain to the class. "I'll be asking questions, and you'll supply the answers."

They agree to that, amidst some laughter.

"Okay," I say, "how are we going to start?"

"Boston," Joe booms out from the back of the room.

"Boston?"

"Yeah," he says. "He's from Boston!"

"No," several women yell. "She's from Boston!"

"That's okay with me"; I ask if it's okay with everyone. They agree.

"Okay." Our subject is a woman from Boston. That's our start point.

"How old is she?" I ask.

"Twenty-four." Several people agree.

"No," I say. When you write a screenplay, you're writing it *for* someone, for a *star*, someone who is "bankable." Faye Dunaway, Jane Fonda, Diane Keaton, Raquel Welch, Candice Bergen, Mia Farrow, Shirley MacLaine, Jill Clayburgh.

We finally decide that she's late twenties—twenty-seven, twenty-eight. We don't want to be *too* specific. If we write it for Jane Fonda, Diane Keaton's going to turn it down.

We move on. "What's her name?"

The name "Sarah" comes into my head, and we go with it.

"Sarah what?"

Sarah Townsend, I decide. A name is a name.

Our start point becomes Sarah Townsend, a twenty-seven-year-old woman from Boston. She is our subject.

Then we create the *context*.

Let's get her personal history. For the sake of simplicity, I'll only give one answer to each question I ask. In class there are several answers given and I select only one. Feel free to disagree with them if you want; make up your own answers, create your own character, your own story.

"What about her parents?" I ask. "Who's her father?"

A doctor, we decide.

Her mother?

A doctor's wife.

What's her father's name?

Lionel Townsend.

What's his background?

We toss a lot of ideas around and finally end up with this: Lionel Townsend belonged to the upper strata of Boston society. Wealthy, smart, conservative, he interrupted medical school at Boston University to serve two years in World War II. After the war he returned home, married, and completed his medical education.

What about Sarah's mother? What was she before she became a doctor's wife?

A teacher. "Elizabeth's her name," someone remarks. Good. Elizabeth might have been teaching when she met Lionel, and she continues teaching grade school during the time he's completing medical school. When he begins his medical practice, she gives up her teaching to become a housewife.

"When did Sarah's parents get married?" I ask.

If Sarah's in her late twenties, her parents must have married after the war—the late 1940s. They've been married almost thirty years. "How'd you figure that out?" someone asks.

"Subtraction," I reply.

What's the relationship between mother and father?

Consistent, and possibly routine. For what it's worth, I add, Sarah's mother's a Capricorn, her father a Libra.

When was Sarah born?

1954. April, an Aries. Does she have any brothers or sisters? No, she's an only child.

Remember, this is a process. For every question asked there are many answers. If you don't agree with them, change them, create your own character.

What kind of childhood did she have?

A lonely one. She wanted brothers and sisters. She was alone most of the time. She probably had a good relationship with her mother until she was in her teens. Then, as always, things went haywire between parent and child.

What's the relationship between Sarah and her father?

Good, but strained. Possibly he wanted a son instead of a daughter; to please her father, Sarah became a tomboy.

This antagonizes her mother, of course. Possibly Sarah is always trying to find a way to please her father, to earn his love and affection. Being a tomboy solves this problem, but creates another one by antagonizing her mother. This will figure later in her relationship to men.

Sarah's family is like all other families, but we're sketching in as much detailed conflict as we can for dramatic purposes.

We're beginning to grasp the dynamics of the Townsend family. So far, there's not been too much disagreement, so we continue to explore the *context* of Sarah Townsend.

I remark that many young women search for their father or father figures throughout their lives. It's interesting to use this as a foundation of character, much in the way that many men search for their mothers in many of the women they meet. Not that it happens all the time. Only that it *does* happen; let's be aware of it so we can possibly use it to our advantage.

There's a lot of discussion about this. I explain when you're creating a character you have to compile nuances of character, so you can choose to use them, or choose not to use them. I tell the class this exercise is based on trial and error. We're going to use what works, and discard what doesn't.

Her mother probably educates Sarah in the ways of the world and, no doubt, cautions her about men. She might tell her daughter, "You can never trust a man. They're only after one thing—your body. They don't like a woman who's too smart." And so on and so on. What Sarah's mother tells her may be true for some of you, or it may not. Use your own experience in creating a character.

At an early age, perhaps Sarah expressed the desire to become a doctor, like her father, and her mother cautioned her against that, saying, "Young girls, especially young girls from Boston, don't become doctors. Either be a social worker, teacher, nurse, secretary, housewife." The 1950s, early '60s, right?

Let's move on. What kind of high school experience did Sarah have?

Active, social, mischievous. She made good grades without having to work very hard for them. She had many friends, and was the leader in rebelling against many of the school's restrictive policies.

Most young people rebel, and Sarah's no exception. She graduates, and decides to go to Radcliffe, which pleases her mother, but majors in political science, which upsets her mother. She's socially active, has an affair with a graduate student in political science, participates in the sit-ins and protests of the '60s. Her actions, based on her rebellious nature, become part of her character—a point of view, an attitude. She graduates from Radcliffe with a degree in political science.

Now what?

She moves to New York to get a job. Her father supports her and is in favor of the move. Her mother does not; she's upset. Sarah's not doing the things she wants her to do—get married and settle down, as befits a "proper young woman from Boston."

Remember, I add, drama is conflict. I explain the relationship between mother and daughter may be used during the screenplay. Or, it may not. Let's see whether it works or not before we make any decision. The writer always operates from the position of choice and responsibility.

Sarah's move to New York is a major crossroads in our creation of character. So far, we've focused on the *context* of Sarah Townsend. Now, we're going to be creating *content.* Let's define the *exterior* forces working on Sarah. Here's the diagram.

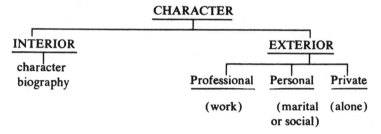

Sarah arrives in New York City in the spring of 1972. What does she do?

Gets an apartment. Her father sends her some money each month, and does not tell her mother; Sarah's on her own and prefers it that way. Then what?

She gets a job. What kind of a job does she get?

Let's discuss that. We know basically the *kind* of person Sarah is; upper-middle-class, independent, free-spirited, rebellious, on her own for the first time and loving it. Committed to herself and her life.

Let's explore the *exterior* forces working on Sarah.

New York, 1972.

Nixon is in the White House. The Vietnam War still rages; the country is in a state of nervous exhaustion. Nixon goes to China. McGovern's gaining in the Presidential primaries and there's hope "he might be the one." George Wallace is gunned down in a shopping center. *The Godfather* is in release.

What kind of job would "fit" Sarah dramatically?

A job working at McGovern headquarters in New York.

This is a point of discussion. We talk about it. Finally, I explain that for me the job satisfies her rebellious nature, it reflects her first independent step away from home. It satisfies her activist political stance and draws on her background as a political science major in college and it gives her parents something to disapprove of. Both of them. We're going after conflict, right?

From now on, through a process of trial and error, we're going to be searching for a theme, or dramatic premise; *something* that will move Sarah into a particular direction to generate a dramatic action. The SUBJECT of a screenplay, remember, is *action* and *character*. We've got the character, now we've got to find the action.

This is a hit-and-miss operation. Things are suggested, changed, rearranged, mistakes are made. I'll say one thing, then contradict myself in the next sentence. Don't worry about it. We're after a specific result—a story: We've got to let ourselves "find" it.

New York. 1972. An election year. Sarah Townsend is working for the McGovern campaign as a paid staff member. Who are her parents voting for?

What does Sarah discover about politics from her experience in the campaign?

That politics aren't necessarily clean or idealistic. Perhaps she discovers something illegal going on—would she do anything about it?

Maybe something happens, I suggest, that creates a major political issue. Perhaps a boyfriend of hers resists the draft and flees to Canada. She might become involved in the movement to bring home the draft resisters.

Remember, we're building a character, creating *context* and *content*, searching for a story that will soon appear. Create a character and a story will emerge.

Someone says Sarah's father has a different point of view

from her—he feels draft resisters are traitors to their country and should be shot. Sarah would argue the opposite; the war is wrong, immoral and illegal; and the people responsible for it, the politicians, should be taken out and shot!

Suddenly, an amazing thing happens in the room. The air becomes tense, heavy with energy as the 50 or so people in the class polarize their *attitudes* and *points of view* about something that happened several years before. The wounds, I realize, are still not healed. We talk about the impact of Vietnam for several minutes. The war is over, we decide. Let's bury it.

Then someone yells out, "Watergate!" Of course! June 1972. Is that a dramatic event that would affect Sarah?

Yes. Sarah would be outraged; it is an event that will generate, or stimulate, a dramatic response. It is a potential "hook" in our, as yet, uncreated, untold, and undefined story. This *is* a creative process, remember, and confusion and contradiction are a part of it.

Two and a half years later, Nixon is gone, the war is almost over, and the issue of amnesty becomes paramount. Sarah, by virtue of her political involvement, has seen and experienced an event firsthand which will guide her to a form of dramatic resolution, as yet, unknown.

A student mentions Sarah might be involved in the movement to bring home draft resisters with complete amnesty. Sarah, we all realize, is a politically motivated person. "Does it work?" is my question. Yes.

Would Sarah be motivated enough to enter law school and become an attorney? I ask.

Everybody responds and we have a lot of discussion about it. Several members of the class don't think it works; they can't relate to it. It's okay. We're writing a screenplay. We need a character who is larger than life; I can see Jane

Fonda, Faye Dunaway, Shirley MacLaine, Vanessa Redgrave, Marsha Mason, Jill Clayburgh, or Diane Keaton in the part of a woman attorney. As the cliché goes, "It's commercial," whatever that means.

At Cinemobile, the first question my boss, Fouad Said, asked me about a script was, "What's it about?" The second question was, "Who's going to star in it?" And I always answered the same thing: Paul Newman, Steve McQueen, Clint Eastwood, Jack Nicholson, Dustin Hoffman, Robert Redford, etc. That satisfied him. You're not writing a screenplay to paper your walls with it. You're writing it, I hope, to sell it!

You may agree or not agree about a woman attorney from Boston as the main character in a movie. My only comment is that it works!

To me, Sarah goes to law school for a specific reason—to help change the political system!

A woman attorney is a good, dramatic choice. Does being a lawyer fit her character? Yes. Let's follow it out, see what happens.

If Sarah is practicing law, something *could* happen, an event or incident that would spark the germ of a story. People start throwing out suggestions. Sarah could be working in military law to aid the draft resisters, one person remarks. Another says she might be working in the area of poverty law. Or business law, or maritime law, or labor relations. An attorney offers a large range of dramatic possibilities.

A woman from Boston remarks that Sarah could be involved in the busing issue. It's a very good idea. We're looking for a dramatic premise, something that will trigger a creative response, a "hook."

That's when it happens—someone mentions he heard a news story about a nuclear power plant. That's it! I realize that's what we've been searching for, the "hook," the jack-pot! Sarah could become involved with a nuclear power plant; perhaps the issue of safety precautions, or lack of them, or the building site, or the political power behind it. This *is* what we've been looking for, I say—an exciting, topical story issue; the "hook," or "gimmick," of our story line. I commit to the choice of Sarah's becoming an attorney.

Everyone agrees. We now expand the exterior forces working on Sarah and begin to fashion our story.

Suppose we take the premise that Sarah Townsend becomes involved with a movement to oppose the construction of nuclear power plants. Perhaps she discovers through an investigation that a particular nuclear plant is unsafe. Politics being what they are, maybe a politician supports the plant despite the fact that it may be unsafe. Like the Karen Silkwood case, someone suggests. Right.

This becomes our story's "hook," or dramatic premise. (If you don't agree, find your own hook!) Now, we have to create, the specifics, the details, the *content*, and we'll have the SUBJECT for a screenplay—an *action* and a *character*.

The screenplay would focus on the subject of the nuclear power plant, which is to be a major political issue in our country, perhaps the world, within the next decade.

What about the story?

Recently, in Pleasanton, California, the authorities closed a nuclear power plant when they discovered it was situated less than 200 feet from a major fault line, the epicenter of an earthquake. Can you imagine what would happen if an earthquake crumbled a nuclear power plant? Try to put your mind around that!

Let's create the opposite point of view. What would her father say about nuclear power plants? "Nuclear energy must work for us," he might say. "In our energy crisis we have to think ahead, develop an energy source for the future; that future is nuclear energy. We just have to insure their safety standards and create rules and guidelines determined by Congress and the Atomic Energy Commission." And, as we all know, those decisions are not always based on reality, but political necessity.

This might be something Sarah accidentally discovers—possibly a political favor that directly relates to an unsafe condition in a nuclear power plant. Now, something's got to happen that will create the dramatic situation.

Someone suggests a person at the nuclear plant could be contaminated and the case is brought to Sarah's law firm, and that's how she becomes involved in the case.

It's a very good suggestion! It becomes the dramatic story line we've been looking for; within the story, a worker becomes contaminated, the case is brought to Sarah's firm, and she's put on the case. The *plot point* at the end of Act I would be when Sarah discovers the worker's contamination, his fatal illness, is caused by unsafe safety procedures; despite threats and obstacles, she decides *to do* something about it.

Act I is the *setup*—we could open with the worker being contaminated. A visually dynamic sequence. The man collapses on the job, is carried out of the plant, an ambulance roars through the streets of Boston. Workers gather, protest; union officials meet and decide to file suit for action that will defend the workers from the unsafe conditions within the plant.

By circumstances, situation, and design, Sarah is chosen to handle the case. Union officials don't like it—she's a woman. The authorities deny her access but she manages to explore the plant anyway; learns about the unsafe conditions. A "brick" is thrown through her window. Threats are made. The law firm can't help her. She goes to the political representatives in charge, is given the runaround, told it's the worker's fault for getting contaminated.

The media start sniffing around. She learns there's a "political connection" between safety standards and plant management. Maybe, someone says, they discover some missing plutonium.

That's the *plot point* at the end of Act I.

Act II is *confrontation*. Sarah confronts obstacle after obstacle in her investigation, so many obstacles that she suspects some kind of political cover-up. She cannot ignore it any longer. We need a "love interest"—perhaps she's involved with a recently divorced attorney with two children. Their relationship becomes strained; he thinks she's "crazy," "paranoid," "hallucinating," and they may not be able to keep it together under the strain.

She will experience conflict and resistance from members of her law firm, she may be told she's going to be removed from the case if she persists in her investigation. Her parents will disagree with her, so she'll have conflict there. The only people who will support and help her are the people who work at the nuclear power plant; they want her to succeed, to publicly expose the unsafe working conditions. We can use the media, and possibly create a reporter who believes she should continue the investigation. He's going to get a story out of it. Possibly there's a romantic link between them.

What about the *plot point* at the end of Act II? It must be an incident or event, remember, that "hooks" into the action and "spins" it around into another direction.

Perhaps the reporter comes to her with definite "proof" that there's been some kind of political favoritism involving many officials. She has the facts in her hands—what is she going to do about it?

Act III is the *resolution*. Sarah, with the help of plant

workers and the media, publicly exposes political favoritism in the government's unsafe regulation of safety standards. The plant is closed until new safety standards are established. Sarah is congratulated on her persistent, courageous, and victorious stand. In other words, we have an "up" ending. Our "heroine" wins!

There are different kinds of endings. In "up" endings, things work out fine. Everybody lives happily ever after, as in *Heaven Can Wait, Rocky, Star Wars,* or *The Turning Point.* In "sad," or "ambiguous," endings "it's up to the audience" to figure out what happens as in *Five Easy Pieces, An Unmarried Woman,* or *F.I.S.T.* In a "down" ending, everybody dies: *The Wild Bunch, Butch Cassidy and the Sundance Kid, Bonnie and Clyde, The Sugarland Express.*

If you're ever in doubt about how to end your story, think in terms of an "up" ending. There are better ways to end your screenplays than have your character caught, shot, captured, die, or be murdered. In the '60s we had "down" endings. The filmgoers of the '70s and '80s wanted "up" endings. Just look at *Star Wars.* It has made more money in a shorter period of time than any other movie in history. And, the two things that run Hollywood are fear and greed.

Resolve your stories with "up" endings!

We put a working title on it: *Precaution!*

Here's our story then: A young woman attorney in Boston discovers unsafe working conditions at a nuclear power plant, and despite political pressure and threats to her life, succeeds in publicly exposing it. The plant is shut down until repairs are made and a safe condition exists.

Not too bad—considering it took us less than an hour to create a character and a story with a strong dramatic premise!

We have an interesting *main character*, Sarah Townsend; an action, uncovering the scandal. We have a beginning, a *plot point* at the end of Act I, potential conflict in the second act, a *plot point* at the end of Act II, and a dramatic resolution.

You may not agree with it or like it—the purpose of the exercise is to set into motion a process, to show you how creating a character generates a dramatic action which uncovers a story.

As I've said, there are two ways to approach a screenplay: Create an idea and "pour" your characters into it, or create a character and let the story emerge out of the character. The second approach is the one we've just used. It all came out of "a young woman from Boston."

∗   ∗   ∗

As an exercise: Try it! See what happens.

6

Endings and Beginnings

*Wherein we establish the importance
of endings and beginnings:*

Question: What's the best way to open your screenplay?

Showing your character at work? In a relationship? Jogging? In bed, alone, or with someone? Driving? Playing golf? At the airport?

Up until now we've discussed abstract principles in writing the screenplay in terms of action and character. At this point, we leave those general concepts behind and move into specific and fundamental components of the screenplay.

Let's backtrack. We began with the idea that a screenplay is like a *noun*—about a *person*, or persons, in a *place*, or places, doing his or her *"thing."* All screenplays have a *subject* and the subject of a screenplay is defined as the *action*, what happens, and the *character,* to whom it happens. There are two kinds of action—*physical* action and *emotional* action; a car chase and a kiss. We discussed character in terms of *dramatic need*, and broke the concept of *character* down into two components—*interior* and *exterior*; your character's life from birth until the movie ends. We talked about *building* character and *creating* character and introduced the idea of *context* and *content*.

Now what? Where do we go from here? What happens next? Look at the *paradigm*:

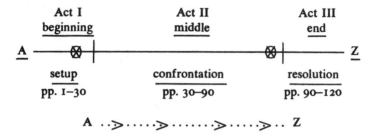

What do you see?

DIRECTION—that's what. Your story *moves forward* from A to Z; from *setup* to *resolution*. Remember the definition of screenplay *structure*: "a linear *progression* of *related* incidents, episodes, and events leading to a dramatic resolution."

That means your story *moves forward* from beginning to end. You've got ten pages (ten minutes) to establish three things to your reader or audience: (1) *who* is your main character? (2) *what* is the dramatic premise—that is, what's it about? and (3) what is the dramatic *situation*—the dramatic circumstances surrounding your story?

So—what's the best way to open your screenplay?

KNOW YOUR ENDING!

What *is* the ending of your story? How is it *resolved*? Does your main character live or die? Get married or divorced? Get away with the holdup, or get caught? Stay on his feet after 15 rounds with Apollo Creed, or not? What is the ending of your screenplay?

A lot of people don't believe you need an ending before you start writing. I hear argument after argument, discussion after discussion, debate after debate. "My characters," people say, "will determine the ending." Or, "My ending grows out of my story." Or, "I'll know my ending when I get to it."

Bullshit!

Those endings usually don't work and are not very effective when they do; often weak, neat, contrived, they are a letdown rather than an emotional shot-in-the-arm. Think of the endings of *Star Wars, Heaven Can Wait,* or *Three Days of the Condor;* strong and conclusive, definitely resolved.

The ending is the first thing you must know before you begin writing.

Why?

It's obvious when you think about it. Your story always moves forward—it follows a path, a direction, a line of development from beginning to end. And *direction* is a *line of development,* the *path along which something lies.*

KNOW YOUR ENDING!

You don't have to know the specific details, but you have to know *what happens.*

I use an example out of my own life to illustrate this.

There was a moment in my life when I didn't know what I wanted to do, or be. I had graduated from high school, my mother had just died, as my father had some years before, and I didn't want to get stuck in some job, or go off to college. I didn't know what I wanted, so I decided to travel around the country. My older brother was in medical school in St. Louis at the time, and I knew I could stay with him or could visit friends in Colorado and New York. So, one morning, I simply got in my car and headed east on Highway 66.

I never knew where I was going till I got there. I preferred it that way. I had good times and bad times, and loved it; I was like a cloud on the wind, drifting without aim or purpose.

I did that for almost two years.

One day, driving through the Arizona desert, I realized I had traveled that same road before. Everything was the same, but different. It was the same mountain in the same barren desert but it was two years later. In reality, I was going nowhere. I spent two years trying to get my head straight, and I still had no purpose, no aim, no goal, no destination, no *direction*. I suddenly saw my future—it was nowhere.

I became aware of time slipping away, almost like an acid trip, and knew I had to "do" something. So I stopped wandering and went back to school. At least I'd have a degree after four years, whatever that meant! Of course, it didn't work out that way—it never does.

When you go on a trip, *you are going someplace*; you have a destination. If I'm going to San Francisco, that's my destination. How I get there is a matter of choice. I can fly, drive, take a bus, a train, ride a motorcycle, a bike, jog, hitchhike, or walk.

I can *choose* how to get there.

The same principle applies to your screenplay. What is the ending of your screenplay? How does your story resolve itself?

Good films are always resolved—one way or another. Think about it.

What's the ending of: *Close Encounters of the Third Kind? Bonnie and Clyde? An Unmarried Woman? Red River? Looking for Mr. Goodbar? Saturday Night Fever? Three Days of the Condor? Alice Doesn't Live Here Anymore? Butch Cassidy and the Sundance Kid? The Treasure of the Sierra Madre? Casablanca? Annie Hall? The Goodbye Girl? Coming Home? Jaws? Heaven Can Wait?*

When you see a well-made film, you'll find a strong and directly stated ending, a definite resolution.

The days of ambiguous endings are over. Vanished. They went out in the 1960s. Today, the audience wants a clear-cut resolution. Do your characters get away, or not? Do they make the relationship work, or don't they? Is the "Death Star" destroyed, the race won or lost?

What is the ending to your screenplay?

And, by ending, I mean resolution. How is it solved? A good illustration is *Chinatown*. There were three drafts of the screenplay, three different endings and two different resolutions.

The first draft of *Chinatown* is much more romantic than the others. Jake Gittes opens and closes the story with a voice-over narration, just the way Raymond Chandler does in most of his stories. When Evelyn Mulwray walks into Jake Gittes' life, he becomes involved with a woman from a different class; she is wealthy, sophisticated, and beautiful and he falls head over heels in love with her. Near the end of the story, when she learns her father, Noah Cross (John Huston) tried to hire Gittes to find her daughter/sister, she realizes he will stop at nothing to get the girl, so she sets out to kill her father. She knows it's the only solution. She phones Noah Cross and tells him to meet her along a deserted part of the coast near San Pedro. When Cross arrives, it is raining heavily, and as he walks up the dirt road looking for his daughter, she jams down her car's accelerator and tries to run him over. He narrowly escapes and races to a marshy area nearby. Evelyn leaves the car, pulls a gun and begins tracking him. Shots are fired. He hides behind a large wooden sign advertising "fresh bait." Evelyn sees him and fires again and again into the sign. Blood mingles with the falling rain, and Noah Cross falls over backwards, dead.

A few moments later, Gittes and Lieutenant Escobar arrive at the scene and then we cut to various shots of modern day Los Angeles and the San Fernando Valley. Gittes, in voice-over narration, tells us Evelyn Mulwray spent four years in prison for killing her father, that he manages to get her daughter/sister safely back to Mexico, and the land scheme Noah Cross so brilliantly conceived results in about 300 million dollars profit. The resolution of this first draft is that justice and order prevail; Noah Cross gets what he deserves, and the graft and corruption of the water scandal is responsible for Los Angeles being what it is today.

That was the first draft.

At that point, Robert Evans, the producer (the man also responsible for *Godfather* and *Love Story*), brought in Roman Polanski as director. Polanski had his own ideas about *Chinatown*. Changes were discussed, then made, and relations between Polanski and Robert Towne, the screenwriter, became tense and strained. They disagreed about many things, mostly about the ending Polanski wanted, in which Noah Cross gets away with murder. The second draft is therefore altered considerably. It is less romantic, the action is trimmed and tightened, and the focus of the resolution changed substantially. The second draft is very close to the final one.

Noah Cross does get away with murder, graft and incest, and now Evelyn Mulwray becomes the innocent victim who pays for her father's crime. Towne's point of view in *Chinatown* is that those who commit certain types of crimes, like murder, robbery, rape or arson, are punished by being sent to prison, but those who commit crimes against an entire community are often rewarded by having streets named after them or plaques dedicated to them at City Hall. Los Angeles literally owes its survival to the water scandal known as The Rape of the Owens Valley; it is the backdrop of the film.

The ending of the second draft now has Gittes planning to meet Evelyn Mulwray in Chinatown; he has arranged for her to be taken to Mexico by Curly (Burt Young), the man in the opening scene, and her daughter/sister is waiting at the boat. Gittes has discovered that Cross is the man behind the murders and water scandal, and when he accuses him, Cross takes him prisoner; they leave for Chinatown. When they arrive, Cross tries to detain Evelyn, but Gittes manages to subdue the older man. Evelyn races to her car only to be blocked by Escobar. Gittes makes a drastic move and lunges at the policeman; during the scuffle, Evelyn drives away. Shots are fired and she is killed, shot in the head.

The last scene shows Noah Cross weeping over Evelyn's body while a stunned Gittes tells Escobar that Cross is the man "responsible" for everything.

The ending in the third draft is modified to accent Towne's point of view, but the resolution is the same as the second draft. Gittes is taken to Chinatown, but Escobar is already there, and arrests the private detective for withholding evidence and puts him in handcuffs. When Evelyn arrives with her daughter/sister, Cross approaches the young girl. Evelyn tells him to stay away, and when he doesn't, she pulls a gun and shoots him in the arm. She gets into her car and drives away. Loach, the cop, fires, and Evelyn is killed, shot through the eye. (Sophocles has Oedipus tear out his eyes when he realizes he committed incest with his mother.)

Horrified by Evelyn's death, Cross puts his arm protectively around his daughter/granddaughter and forcefully whisks her away into the darkness.

Noah Cross gets away with it all; murder, the water scandal, the girl. "You gotta be rich to kill somebody, anybody, and get away with it," Gittes tells Curly in the opening scene.

The *resolution* must be clear in your mind before you write one word on paper; it is a *context*, it *holds* the ending in place.

The same principle applies to a recipe. When you cook something, you don't throw things together and then see what you've got! You know what you're going to cook before you go into the kitchen; all you have to do is cook it!

Your story is like a journey, the ending its destination. Both are related.

Cat Stevens sums it up in his song *Sitting:*

> *Life is like a maze of doors,*
> *and they open from the side you're on.*
> *Just keep on pushin' hard, boy, try as you may,*
> *you might wind up where you started from.*

The Chinese say "the longest journey begins with the first step," and in many philosophical systems "endings and beginnings" are connected; as in the concept of Yin and Yang, two concentric circles joined together, forever united, forever opposed. Endings and beginnings are related, and the principle can be applied to the screenplay. *Rocky* is a case in point. The film opens with Rocky fighting an opponent; it ends with him fighting Apollo Creed for the Heavyweight Championship of the World.

In life, the ending of one thing is usually the beginning of something else. If you're single and get married, you're ending one way of life and beginning another. If you're married, then get divorced or separated or become widowed, the same principle holds true; you're going from living with someone to living alone. An ending is always a beginning, and a beginning is really an ending. Everything is related in the screenplay, as in life.

If you can find a way to illustrate this in your screenplay, it is to your advantage. *The Sugarland Express*, written by Hal Barwood and Matthew Robbins, does this well.

The film opens at the crossroads of a two-lane highway. A Greyhound bus pulls to a stop and Goldie Hawn gets out and walks up the road as the credits begin.

The story progresses. She breaks her husband out of a detention center to kidnap their child from its foster parents; they take a highway patrolman hostage, then proceed to be hunted down by the law and ultimately, he is killed. (Beginning, middle, and end, right?)

A shootout ends the film. The camera pans and the last shot is a crossroads on a two-lane highway. An empty highway opens the film and an empty highway closes it.

The Hustler opens with Paul Newman arriving to play pool with Minnesota Fats; it ends with Newman leaving the pool hall after winning the game, a self-imposed exile from the world of pool. The film opens with a pool game and closes with a pool game.

In *Three Days of the Condor*, Robert Redford's first line raises the dramatic premise of the entire film: "Anything in the pouch for me, Dr. Lapp?" The answer to that question results in several people being brutally murdered, and Redford almost losing his life. He has uncovered a "CIA" within the CIA—and, he doesn't know it until the end of the movie. His discovery is the final key that resolves the movie.

The ending of *Condor*, by Lorenzo Semple, Jr., and David Rayfiel, from the novel *Six Days of the Condor* by James Grady, is an excellent example of story resolution. Ably directed by Sydney Pollack, it is a fast-moving, well-constructed thriller that works on all levels—the acting is excellent, the cinematography effective, the editing tight and lean; there is no "fat" in the film. It's one of my favorite teaching films, and fits the *paradigm* perfectly.

By the end of the movie, Redford has tracked down the mysterious Lionel Atwood—a high-level executive in the CIA—but he doesn't know *who* Atwood is or what his connection is, if any, to the murders committed. In the "resolution scene," Redford establishes that Atwood is the man who ordered the murders; that he is responsible for establishing a secret cell of the CIA within the CIA because of the world "oil fields." This established, Max von Sydow appears, the hired assassin of the intelligence underworld, and abruptly kills Atwood. He is now back in the employ of the "company," the CIA. Redford breathes easier; he's alive. "At least for now," von Sydow reminds him.

No loose ends. Everything is resolved dramatically, in terms of action and character; all questions raised are answered. The story is complete.

The filmmakers added a "tag" scene at the end. Robert

Redford and Cliff Robertson are standing in front of the New York Times Building, and Redford states that if anything happens to him, the *Times* has the story. But "will they print it?" Robertson asks.

It's a good question.

Fade out. The end.

The "tag" scene is not the resolution of the film; it simply states a dramatic point of view. It's "our" government, the movie says: We, the people, have the right to know what goes on within the trappings of government.

We must exercise it.

Endings and beginnings; two sides of the same coin.

Choose and structure and dramatize your ending carefully. If you can relate your beginning and ending, it adds a nice cinematic touch. Open with a scene on a river and end it on the ocean; water to water. Or highway to highway, sunrise to sunset. Sometimes you'll be able to do it, sometimes not. See if it works; if it does, use it; if not, junk it.

When you know your ending you can effectively choose your opening.

What *is* the opening of your screenplay? How does it begin? What do you write after FADE IN:?

If you've determined your ending you can choose an incident or event that leads you to the end. You might reveal your main character at work, at play, alone or with someone, either business or pleasure. What happens in the first scene of the film? Where does it take place?

There are several ways to open your screenplay. You can "grab" the audience with a visually exciting action sequence, as *Star Wars* does. Or, you can create an interesting character introduction as Robert Towne does in *Shampoo*: a darkened bedroom, moans and squeals of pleasurable delight —the phone rings, loud, insistent, shattering the mood. It's another woman—for Warren Beatty, who's in bed with Lee Grant. It shows us everything we need to know about his character.

Shakespeare is a master of openings. Either he opens with an *action* sequence, like the ghost walking the parapet in *Hamlet*, or the witches in *Macbeth*, or he uses a scene revealing something about the character: Richard III is hunchbacked and laments about the "winter of our discontent"; Lear demands to know how much his daughters love him, in terms of dollars and cents. Before *Romeo and Juliet* begins the chorus appears, bangs for silence, and synopsizes the story of the "star-crossed lovers."

Shakespeare knew his audience; the groundlings standing in the pit, the poor and oppressed, drinking freely, talking boisterously to the performers if they didn't like the action on stage. He had to "grab" their attention and focus it on the action.

An opening can be visually active and exciting, grabbing the audience immediately. Another kind of opening is expository, slower-paced in establishing character and situation.

Your story determines the type of opening you choose.

The Watergate break-in opens *All the President's Men;* it is a tense and exciting sequence. *Close Encounters of the Third Kind* opens with a dynamic, mysterious sequence because we don't know what's going on. *Julia* is moody, reflective, establishing character wound within in the strands of memory. *An Unmarried Woman* opens with an argument, then *reveals* the life of the *married* woman, Jill Clayburgh.

Choose your opening well. You've got ten pages to grab the reader, or audience; if you open with an action sequence as in *Rocky,* keep it under eight pages and then set up your story.

Where to put the "credits" is a film decision, not a writing one. Determining the placement of credits is the last thing done on a film, and it's the decision of the film editor and director. Whether it's a dynamic credit montage, or simply white cards superimposed on a black background, credits are not your decision. You can write "credits begin," or "credits end" if you want, but that's it. Write the screenplay, don't worry about the credits.

"The first ten pages"

The first ten pages of your screenplay are absolutely the most crucial. Within the first ten pages a reader will know whether your story is working or not; whether it's been set up or not. That's the reader's job.

As head of the story department at Cinemobile, I was always 70 scripts behind. The pile on my desk was rarely smaller. When I was almost caught up, a stack of scripts suddenly appeared from nowhere—from agents, producers, directors, actors, studios. I read so many screenplays that were boring and poorly written I could tell within the first ten pages whether the script was set up correctly. I gave the writer 30 pages to set up the story; if it wasn't done by then I reached for the next script on the pile. I had too many to read to waste my time reading a script that didn't work. I was reading three scripts a day. I didn't have time to *hope* the writer did his job; he either set up his story or he didn't. If he didn't, I threw the script into the large trash bin that served as the "return file."

"That's showbiz."

Nobody sells a script in Hollywood without the help of a reader. In Hollywood, "nobody reads"; producers don't read, readers read. There is an elaborate filtering system regarding screenplays in this town. Everybody says they're going to read your script over the weekend, and that means they're going to give it to somebody to read within the next few weeks; a reader, a secretary, a receptionist, a wife, girlfriend, assistant. If the "reader" says she "likes" the screenplay, the person will get another opinion or scan the first few pages himself, ten pages, to be exact.

You've got ten pages to grab your reader. What are you going to do with them?

I tell everyone in my screenwriting class they should be seeing as many movies as possible. At least two movies a week. In movie theaters. If you can't afford that, at least one movie in a theater and one on TV.

It's very important for you to see movies. All kinds of movies; good films, bad films, foreign films, old films, new films. Every film you see becomes a learning experience; if you examine it, it will generate a process giving you an expanded awareness of the screenplay. A movie should be viewed as a working session; talk about it, discuss it, see whether it fits the *paradigm* or not.

When you go to a movie, for example, how long does it take you to make a decision about whether you like it or not? After the lights fade, and the movie begins, how long does it take you to make a decision, either consciously or unconsciously, about whether the movie is worth the price of admission?

And you *do* make that decision, whether you're aware of it or not.

You already know the answer.

Ten minutes. Within the first ten minutes you're going to make a decision about the film you're seeing. Check it out. The next time you go to a movie notice how long it takes you to decide whether you like it or not. Look at your watch.

Ten minutes is ten pages. Your reader or audience is either going to be with you, or not. How you build and structure your opening is going to influence the reaction of the reader and viewer.

You've got ten pages to establish three things: (I) *who* is your main character? (2) *what* is the dramatic premise—that is, what's your story about? and (3) what is the dramatic *situation* of your screenplay—the dramatic circumstances surrounding your story?

Citizen Kane illustrates this perfectly. The film opens with Charles Foster Kane (Orson Welles) dying alone in his large palace called Xanadu. He holds a toy paperweight in his hand. It rolls out of his hand onto the floor and the camera lingers on the paperweight showing a boy with a sled, and over this we hear Kane's dying words: "Rosebud . . . Rosebud."

Who is Rosebud? *What* is Rosebud? The answer to that question is the subject of the movie. It could be called an "emotional detective story." The life of Charles Foster Kane is revealed by the reporter trying to find the meaning and significance of "Rosebud."

The last shot of the movie shows a sled burning in the giant incinerator; as the flames devour it we see the word "Rosebud" appear, symbolizing the lost childhood that Charles Foster Kane gave up to become what he was.

You've got ten pages to "grab" your reader and 30 pages to set up your story.

Endings and beginnings are essential to a well-constructed screenplay. What's the best way to open your screenplay? KNOW YOUR ENDING!

∗   ∗   ∗

As an exercise: Determine the ending of your screenplay, then design your opening. The primary rule for the opening is: Does it work? Does it set your story in motion? Does it establish your main character? Does it state the dramatic premise? Does it set up the situation? Does it set up a problem that your character must confront and overcome; does it state your character's need?

7

The Setup

Wherein we discuss the importance
of the first ten pages of
Chinatown:

Everything is related in a screenplay, so it becomes essential to introduce your story components from the beginning. You've got ten pages to grab or hook your reader, so you've got to set up your story immediately.

That means page one, word one. The reader must know what's going on immediately. Tricks or gimmicks don't work. You've got to set up the story information in a visual way. The reader must know *who* the main character is, *what* the dramatic *premise* is, that is, what it's about, and, the dramatic *situation*—the circumstances surrounding the action.

These three elements must be introduced within the first ten pages, or immediately following an action sequence like the opening of *Raiders of the Lost Ark*. I tell students in my workshops and seminars that you must approach the first ten pages of your screenplay as a *unit,* or *block,* of dramatic action. It is the unit that sets up everything to follow, and therefore must be designed and executed with efficiency and good, solid dramatic value.

There is no better illustration of this than Robert Towne's screenplay of *Chinatown*. Towne is a master at setting up his story and characters. It is textured with skill and precision, layer by layer, and the more I read the script, the more I learn how good it really is.

As far as I'm concerned, *Chinatown* is the best American screenplay written during the 1970s. Not that it's better than *Godfather I* or *Apocalypse Now* or *All the President's Men* or *Close Encounters of the Third Kind,* but as a reading experience the story, visual dynamics, backdrop, backstory, subtext of "Chinatown" are woven together to create a solid dramatic unity of a story told with pictures.

The first time I saw the film, I was bored, tired, and dozed off during the screening. It seemed a very cold and distant film. I saw it again and felt it was a good film, but nothing spectacular. Then, in a class at Sherwood Oaks, I read the screenplay. It blew me away. The characterizations, the style of writing, the movement, the flow of the story are flawless.

Recently, I was invited by the Ministry of Dutch Culture and the Belgium Film Industry to teach a screenwriting workshop in Brussels, and I took *Chinatown* with me to use as a teaching example. The workshop was attended by film professionals and students from Belgium, France, Holland, and England; together we viewed, read, and analyzed the script in terms of structure and story. It was a profound learning experience. I thought I knew the script perfectly, but I learned I hardly knew it at all. What makes it so good is that it works on *all* levels—story, structure, characterization, visuals—yet everything we need to know is set up within the first ten pages. It is a *unit* or *block* of dramatic action.

Chinatown is about a private detective who is hired by the wife of a prominent man to find out who he's having an affair with, and in the process becomes involved in several murders and uncovers a major water scandal.

The first ten pages set up the entire screenplay. What follows are the first ten pages of *Chinatown* as they appear in the screenplay. Read it carefully. Notice how Towne sets up his *main character,* how he introduces the dramatic premise, reveals the dramatic situation.

(NOTE: All questions about screenplay form will be discussed in Chapter 13.)

(page 1 of screenplay)

CHINATOWN

by Robert Towne

FADE IN

FULL SCREEN PHOTOGRAPH

grainy but unmistakably a man and woman making love. Photograph shakes. SOUND of a man MOANING in anguish. The photograph is dropped, REVEALING another, more compromising one. Then another, and another. More moans.

>   CURLY'S VOICE
>   *(crying out)*
> Oh, no.

INT. GITTES' OFFICE

CURLY drops the photos on Gittes' desk. Curly towers over GITTES and sweats heavily through his workman's clothes, his breathing progressively more labored. A drop plunks on Gittes' shiny desktop.

Gittes notes it. A fan whirrs overhead. Gittes glances up at it. He looks cool and brisk in a white linen suit despite the heat.

Never taking his eyes off Curly, he lights a cigarette using a lighter with a "nail" on his desk.

Curly, with another anguished sob, turns and rams his fist into the wall, kicking the wastebasket as he does. He starts to sob again, slides along the wall where his fist has left a noticeable dent and its impact has sent the signed photos of several movie stars askew.

Curly slides on into the blinds and sinks to his knees. He is weeping heavily now, and is in such pain that he actually bites into the blinds.

Gittes doesn't move from his chair.

> GITTES
>
> All right, enough is enough—you can't eat the Venetian blinds, Curly. I just had 'em installed on Wednesday.

Curly responds slowly, rising to his feet, crying. Gittes reaches into his desk and pulls out a shot glass, quickly selects a cheaper bottle of bourbon from several fifths of more expensive whiskeys.

Gittes pours a large shot. He shoves the glass across his desk toward Curly.

(2)

> GITTES
>
> —Down the hatch.

Curly stares dumbly at it. Then picks it up, and drains it. He sinks back into the chair opposite Gittes, begins to cry quietly.

CURLY
(drinking, relaxing a little)
She's just no good.

GITTES
What can I tell you, kid? You're right. When
you're right, you're right, and you're right.

CURLY
—Ain't worth thinking about.

Gittes leaves the bottle with Curly.

GITTES
You're absolutely right, I wouldn't give her another thought.

CURLY
(pouring himself)
You know, you're *okay*, Mr. Gittes. I know it's
your job, but you're okay.

GITTES
(settling back, breathing a little easier)
Thanks, Curly. Call me Jake.

CURLY
Thanks. You know something, Jake?

GITTES
What's that, Curly?

CURLY
I think I'll kill her.

INT. DUFFY & WALSH'S OFFICE

noticeably less plush than Gittes'. A well-groomed, dark-haired WOMAN sits nervously between their two desks, fiddling with the veil on her pillbox hat.

> WOMAN
> —I was hoping Mr. Gittes could see to this personally—

> WALSH
> *(almost the manner of someone comforting the bereaved)*
> —If you'll allow us to complete our preliminary questioning, by then he'll be free.

There is the SOUND of ANOTHER MOAN coming from Gittes' office—something made of glass shatters. The Woman grows more edgy.

INT. GITTES' OFFICE—GITTES & CURLY

Gittes and Curly stand in front of the desk, Gittes staring contemptuously at the heavy breathing hulk towering over him. Gittes takes a handkerchief and wipes away the plunk of perspiration on his desk.

> CURLY
> *(crying)*
> They don't kill a guy for that.

> GITTES
> Oh they don't?

> CURLY
> Not for your wife. That's the unwritten law.

Gittes pounds the photos on the desk, shouting:

GITTES

I'll tell you the unwritten law, you dumb son of a bitch, you gotta be rich to kill somebody, anybody, and get away with it. You think you got that kind of dough, you think you got that kind of class?

(4)

Curly shrinks back a little.

CURLY

...No...

GITTES

You bet your ass you don't. You can't even pay me off.

This seems to upset Curly even more.

CURLY

I'll pay the rest next trip—we only caught sixty ton of skipjack around San Benedict. We hit a chubasco, they don't pay you for skipjack the way they do tuna or albacore—

GITTES

(easing him out of his office)

Forget it. I only mention it to illustrate a point...

INT. OFFICE RECEPTION

He's now walking him past SOPHIE, who pointedly averts her gaze. He opens the door where on the pebbled glass can be read: J.J. GITTES and Associates—DISCREET IN-VESTIGATION.

GITTES

I don't want your last dime.

He throws an arm around Curly and flashes a dazzling smile.

GITTES
(continuing)
What kind of a guy do you think I am?

CURLY

Thanks, Mr. Gittes.

GITTES
Call me Jake. Careful driving home, Curly.

He shuts the door on him and the smile disappears.

(5)

He shakes his head, starting to swear under his breath.

SOPHIE
—A Mrs. Mulwray is waiting for you, with Mr. Walsh and Mr. Duffy.

Gittes nods, walks on in.

INT. DUFFY & WALSH'S OFFICE

Walsh rises when Gittes enters.

WALSH
Mrs. Mulwray, may I present Mr. Gittes?

Gittes walks over to her and again flashes a warm, sympathetic smile.

GITTES
How do you do, Mrs. Mulwray?

MRS. MULWRAY
Mr. Gittes . . .

GITTES
Now, Mrs. Mulwray, what seems to be the problem?

She holds her breath. The revelation isn't easy for her.

MRS. MULWRAY
My husband, I believe, is seeing another woman.

Gittes looks mildly shocked. He turns for confirmation to his two partners.

GITTES
(gravely)
No, really?

MRS. MULWRAY
I'm afraid so.

GITTES
I am sorry.

Gittes pulls up a chair, sitting next to Mrs. Mulwray—between Duffy and Walsh. Duffy cracks his gum.

(6)

Gittes gives him an irritated glance. Duffy stops chewing.

MRS. MULWRAY
Can't we talk about this alone, Mr. Gittes?

                    GITTES
I'm afraid not, Mrs. Mulwray. These men are
my operatives and at some point they're going to
assist me. I can't do everything myself.

                    MRS. MULWRAY
Of course not.

                    GITTES
Now—what makes you certain he is involved
with someone?

Mrs. Mulwray hesitates. She seems uncommonly nervous at
the question.

                    MRS. MULWRAY
—a wife can tell.

Gittes sighs.

                    GITTES
Mrs. Mulwray, do you love your husband?

                    MRS. MULWRAY
                    (shocked)
. . . Yes, of course.

                    GITTES
                    (deliberately)
Then go home and forget about it.

                    MRS. MULWRAY
—but . . .

                    GITTES
                    (staring intently at her)
I'm sure he loves you, too. You know the expres-
sion, "let sleeping dogs lie"? You're better off
not knowing.

MRS. MULWRAY
(with some real anxiety)
But I have to know!

Her intensity is genuine. Gittes looks to his two partners.

GITTES
All right, what's your husband's first name?

MRS. MULWRAY
Hollis. Hollis Mulwray.

GITTES
(visibly surprised)
—Water and Power?

Mrs. Mulwray nods, almost shyly. Gittes is now casually but carefully checking out the detailing of Mrs. Mulwray's dress —her handbag, shoes, etc.

MRS. MULWRAY
—he's the Chief Engineer.

DUFFY
(a little eagerly)
—*Chief* Engineer?

Gittes' glance tells Duffy Gittes wants to do the questioning. Mrs. Mulwray nods.

GITTES
(confidentially)
This type of investigation can be hard on your pocketbook, Mrs. Mulwray. It takes time.

MRS. MULWRAY
Money doesn't matter to me, Mr. Gittes.

Gittes sighs.

>   GITTES
>   Very well. We'll see what we can do.

EXT. CITY HALL—MORNING

already shimmering with heat.

(8)

A drunk blows his nose with his fingers into the fountain at
the foot of the steps.

Gittes, impeccably dressed, passes the drunk on the way up
the stairs.

INT. COUNCIL CHAMBERS

Former Mayor SAM BAGBY is speaking. Behind him is a
huge map, with overleafs and bold lettering:
     "PROPOSED ALTO VALLEJO DAM AND RESERVOIR"
Some of the councilmen are reading funny papers and gossip
columns while Bagby is speaking.

>   BAGBY
>   —Gentlemen, today you can walk out that door,
>   turn right, hop on a streetcar and in twenty-five
>   minutes end up smack in the Pacific Ocean. Now
>   you can swim in it, you can fish in it, you can
>   sail in it—but you can't drink it, you can't water
>   your lawns with it, you can't irrigate an orange
>   grove with it. Remember—we live next door to
>   the ocean but we also live on the edge of the
>   desert. Los Angeles is a desert community. Be-
>   neath this building, beneath every street, there's
>   a desert. Without water the dust will rise up and
>   cover us as though we'd never existed!
>   *(pausing, letting the implication sink in)*

CLOSE—GITTES

sitting next to some grubby farmers, bored. He yawns—edges away from one of the dirtier farmers.

> BAGBY (O.S.)
> *(continuing)*
> The Alto Vallejo can save us from that, and I respectfully suggest that eight and a half million dollars is a fair price to pay to keep the desert from our streets—and not on top of them.

(9)

AUDIENCE—COUNCIL CHAMBERS

An amalgam of farmers, businessmen, and city employees have been listening with keen interest. A couple of the farmers applaud. Somebody shooshes them.

COUNCIL COMMITTEE

in a whispered conference.

> COUNCILMAN
> *(acknowledging Bagby)*
> —Mayor Bagby . . . let's hear from the departments again—I suppose we better take Water and Power first. Mr. Mulwray.

REACTION—GITTES

looking up with interest from his racing form.

MULWRAY

walks to the huge map with overleafs. He is a slender man in his sixties who wears glasses and moves with surprising fluidity. He turns to a smaller, younger man, and nods. The man turns the overleaf on the map.

> MULWRAY
> In case you've forgotten, gentlemen, over five hundred lives were lost when the Van der Lip Dam gave way—core samples have shown that beneath this bedrock is shale similar to the permeable shale in the Van der Lip disaster. It couldn't withstand that kind of pressure there.
>
> *(referring to a new overleaf)*
> Now you propose yet another dirt-banked terminus dam with slopes of two and one half to one, one hundred twelve feet high and a twelve-thousand-acre water surface. Well, it won't hold. I won't build it. It's that simple—I am not making that kind of mistake twice. Thank you, gentlemen.

(10)

Mulwray leaves the overleaf board and sits down. Suddenly there are some whoops and hollers from the rear of the chambers and a red-faced FARMER drives in several scrawny, bleating sheep. Naturally, they cause a commotion.

> COUNCIL PRESIDENT
> *(shouting to farmer)*
> What in the hell do you think you're doing?

(as the sheep bleat down the aisles
toward the Council)
Get those goddam things out of here!

FARMER
(right back)
Tell me where to take them! You don't have an
answer for that so quick, do you?

Bailiffs and sergeants-at-arms respond to the imprecations of
the Council and attempt to capture the sheep and the farmers,
having to restrain one who looks like he's going to bodily
attack Mulwray.

FARMER
(through above, to Mulwray)
—You steal the water from the Valley, ruin the
grazing, starve my livestock—who's paying you
to do that, Mr. Mulwray, that's what I want to
know!

OMITTED

The scene ends and we cut to the Los Angeles River bed
where Gittes watches Mulwray through binoculars.

∗　　∗　　∗

Let's take a look at the first ten pages:
The main character, Jake Gittes (Jack Nicholson), is introduced in his office, showing photographs of Curly's wife
being unfaithful.

We learn things about Gittes. On page 1, for example, we find that he "looks cool and brisk in a white linen suit despite the heat." He is shown to be a meticulous man who uses his "handkerchief to wipe away the plunk of perspiration on his desk."' When he walks up the steps of City Hall a few pages later, he is "impeccably dressed." These *visual* descriptions convey character traits that reflect his personality. Notice how Gittes is *not physically described* at all; he's not tall, thin, fat, short, or anything else. He seems like a nice guy. "I wouldn't take your last dime," he says. "What kind of a guy do you think I am?" Yet, he offers Curly a drink from a "cheaper bottle of bourbon from the several fifths of more expensive whiskeys." He's vulgar, yet exudes a certain amount of charm and sophistication. He's the kind of man who wears monogrammed shirts and silk handkerchiefs, and has his shoes shined and hair cut at least once a week.

On page 4, Towne reveals the dramatic situation *visually* in the stage directions: "on the pebbled glass can be read J.J. GITTES and Associates—DISCREET INVESTIGATION." Gittes is a private detective who specializes in divorce work, or "other people's dirty linen" as the cop Loach says about him. Later we'll learn he's an ex-cop who left the force and has mixed feelings about cops; when Escobar tells him he made lieutenant after Gittes left Chinatown, the private detective suffers a twinge of envy.

The dramatic premise is established on page 5 (five minutes into the film), when the phony Mrs. Mulwray (Diane Ladd) informs Jake Gittes, "My husband, I believe, is seeing another woman." That statement sets up everything to follow: Gittes, the ex-cop, "checks out the detailing of Mrs. Mulwray's dress—her handbag, shoes, etc." That's his job, and he's very good at what he does.

When Gittes tracks down and takes pictures of "the little twist" Mulwray is supposedly having an affair with, as far as he is concerned, the case is closed. The next day he's surprised to find the pictures he took on the front page of the newspaper with headlines declaring that the head of the Department of Water and Power has been "caught" in a love nest. He doesn't know how his pictures got into the paper. When he returns to his office he is further surprised to find the *real* Mrs. Mulwray (Faye Dunaway) there to greet him, the plot point at the end of Act I.

"Do you know me?" she asks.

"No," Gittes replies. "I would have remembered."

"Since you agree we've never met, you must also agree that I haven't hired you to do anything—certainly not spy on my husband," she says. As she leaves, her attorney hands Gittes a complaint that could take his license away and smear his name and reputation.

Gittes doesn't know what's going on. If Faye Dunaway is the *real* Mrs. Mulwray, *who* was the woman who hired him and *why*? More important, *who* hired the woman to hire him? Somebody, he doesn't know who or why, has gone to a lot of trouble to set him up. And nobody sets up Jake Gittes! He's going to find out who's responsible and why. That is Jake Gittes' dramatic need, and it drives him through the story until he solves the mystery.

The dramatic premise—"My husband, I believe, is seeing another woman"—sets up the *direction* of the screenplay. And, direction, remember, is "a line of development."

Gittes accepts the case, and finds Hollis Mulwray at City Hall. In the council chambers, a discussion is in progress about the proposed Alto Vallejo dam and reservoir.

In an interview I did with Robert Towne at Sherwood

Oaks, he said he approached *Chinatown* from the point of view that "some crimes are punished because they can be punished. If you kill somebody, rob or rape somebody, you'll be caught and thrown into jail. But crimes against an entire community you really can't punish, so you end up rewarding them. You know, those people who get their names on streets and plaques at City Hall. And that's the basic point of view of the story."

"You know something, Jake?" Curly tells Gittes on page 2, "I think I'll kill her [his wife]."

Gittes responds with the prophetic lines that illustrate Towne's point of view. "You gotta be rich to kill somebody, anybody, and get away with it. You think you got that kind of dough, you think you got that kind of class?" (Ironically, this is one of the scenes cut out when the film was trimmed for television.)

Curly certainly can't get away with murder, but Noah Cross (John Huston), Evelyn Mulwray's father and former head of the Department of Water and Power along with Hollis Mulwray, can and does get away with it. The ending of the film shows John Huston whisking his daughter/granddaughter into the night after Faye Dunaway is killed trying to escape. That is Towne's point of view: "You gotta be rich to kill somebody, anybody, and get away with it."

That brings us to the "crime" of *Chinatown,* a scheme based on the water scandal known as The Rape of the Owens Valley. It is the backdrop of *Chinatown.*

In 1900, the city of Los Angeles, "a desert community" as former mayor Bagby reminds us, was growing and expanding so fast it was literally running out of water. If the city was to survive, it had to find another source of water. L.A. is right next door to the Pacific Ocean. "You can swim in it, you can fish in it, you can sail on it, but you can't drink it, you can't water your lawns with it, and you can't irrigate an orange grove with it," Bagby argues.

The closest water to L.A. is the Owens River, located in the Owens Valley, a green and fertile area about 250 miles northeast of Los Angeles. A group of businessmen, community leaders, and politicians—some call them "men of vision" —saw the need for water and conceived a marvelous scheme. They would buy up the river rights of the Owens River, by force if necessary, then buy up all that worthless land in the San Fernando Valley, about 20 miles outside L.A. Then they would place a bond issue on the ballot that would fund building an aqueduct from the Owens Valley across 250 miles of blazing desert and jagged foothills to the San Fernando Valley. Then they would turn around and sell the now "fertile" land of the San Fernando Valley to the city of Los Angeles for an enormous sum of money; about 300 million dollars.

That was the plan. The government knew about it, the newspapers knew about it, the local politicians all knew about it. When the time was right, the authorities would "influence" the people of Los Angeles to pass the proposed bond issue.

In 1906, a drought fell upon Los Angeles. Things got bad, then worse. People were forbidden to wash their cars or water their lawns; they couldn't flush their toilets more than a few times a day. The city dried up; flowers died, lawns turned brown, and scare headlines declared "Los Angeles is dying of thirst!" "Save our City!"

To underscore the drastic need for water during the drought and to make certain the citizens passed the bond issue, the Department of Water and Power dumped thousands of gallons of water into the ocean.

When it came time to vote, the bond issue passed easily. The Owens Valley aqueduct took several years to complete.

When it was finished, William Mulholland, then head of the Department of Water and Power, turned the water over to the city: "There it is," he said. "Take it." Los Angeles flourished and grew like wildfire, the Owens Valley withered and died. No wonder it was called The Rape of the Owens Valley.

Robert Towne took this scandal that occurred in 1906 and used it as the backdrop in *Chinatown*. He changed the time period from the turn of the century to 1937, when the visual elements of Los Angeles had the classic and distinctive look of Southern California.

The water scandal is woven through the screenplay, and Gittes uncovers it a piece at a time. That's why it's such a great film. *Chinatown* is a voyage of discovery. We learn things at the same time Jake Gittes learns them. Audience and character are linked together, piecing together bits and pieces of information, and putting them together. It *is* a detective story, after all.

When I was conducting the workshop in Brussels, I had an amazing insight into *Chinatown*. I had read the script and seen the movie maybe a half dozen times, but there was still something about it that was bothering me. I had a feeling I was missing something, something I couldn't put into words, something important. While I was in Brussels, I was taken to several of the marvelous art museums of Belgium and got turned on to a group of fifteenth and sixteenth century painters known as the Flemish Primitives: Bosch, Jan van Eyck, Breughel, painters who paved the way and laid down the foundations of modern art.

One weekend I was visiting Bruges, a marvelous fifteenth century city filled with wonderful architecture and canals, and I was taken to a museum featuring early Flemish art. My friend casually pointed out a certain painting. It was bright, colorful and showed two people (the patrons) in the foreground, standing against a beautiful landscape of rolling hills and the sea. It was beautiful. She told me the background I admired was really an Italian landscape. I was surprised and asked her how she knew. She explained it was the custom of the early Flemish painters to travel to Italy to sharpen their skills, to study color and texture, and refine their technique. They sketched and painted Italian landscapes, and then returned to Brussels or Antwerp. When they painted their patrons, they used these landscapes as "backdrops" for their paintings. The paintings are remarkable in style and content.

I looked at that particular painting for a long time, at the patrons in the foreground, admiring the Italian landscape in the background. That's when the light bulb flashed, and suddenly I understood *Chinatown*! I finally understood what had been nagging me about the film. Robert Towne took a scandal that occurred at the turn of the century and used it as the backdrop for a screenplay that takes place in 1937! That's what the Flemish painters did!

That's film! It is a cinematic process that enriches the story.

That's when I knew I had to know more about the Owens Valley. So I researched Bob Towne's research. I learned the origin, background, and facts of the Owens Valley scandal. The next time I read the script and saw the film it was like seeing it for the first time.

The water scandal that Noah Cross conceives and executes, the crime that causes the deaths of Hollis Mulwray, Leroy the drunk, Ida Sessions, and finally Evelyn Mulwray, the scandal that Jake Gittes uncovers, is woven with great subtlety and skill throughout the entire screenplay, like a fifteenth century Belgian tapestry.

And Noah Cross gets away with murder.

All this is established and set up on page 8 when Gittes is in the council chambers, and we hear Bagby arguing that "eight-and-a-half million dollars is a fair price to pay to keep the deserts from our streets—and not on top of them."

Mulwray, the character modeled on William Mulholland,

replies the dam site is unsafe as proven by the previous Van der Lip Dam disaster and says, "I won't build it. It's that simple—I am not making that kind of mistake twice." By refusing to build the dam, Hollis Mulwray becomes a target for murder; he is an obstacle that must be eliminated.

Again, on page 10, the dramatic question of the screenplay is raised: "You steal the water from the Valley, ruin the grazing, starve my livestock—" yells the farmer who invades the chambers. "Who's paying you to do that, Mr. Mulwray, that's what I want to know!"

So does Gittes.

It is *the* question that propels the story to its final resolution and it is all *set up* from the very beginning, in the first ten pages, and moves in a *linear* direction to the end.

By introducing the main character, stating the dramatic premise, creating the dramatic situation, the screenplay moves with precision and skill to its conclusion.

"Either you bring the water to L.A., or you bring L.A. to the water," Noah Cross tells Gittes.

That is the foundation of the entire story. That's what makes it so great.

It's that simple.

*   *   *

As an exercise: Reread the first ten pages of *Chinatown*. See how the backdrop of the action, the scandal, is introduced. See if you can design your opening ten pages in such a way that you introduce the main character, state the dramatic premise, and sketch the dramatic situation in the most cinematic way.

8

The Sequence

Wherein we discuss the dynamics of the sequence:

"Synergy" is the study of systems; the behavior of systems as a whole, independent of their working parts. R. Buckminster Fuller, the noted scientist and humanitarian, creator of the geodesic dome, stresses the concept of synergy as the *relationship* between the whole and its parts; that is, a system.

The screenplay is comprised of a series of elements that can be compared to a "system"; a number of individually related parts arranged to form a unity, or whole; the *solar system* is composed of nine planets orbiting the sun; the *circulatory system* works in conjunction with all the organs of the body; a *stereo system* is made up of amplifier, preamp, tuner, turntable, speakers, cartridge, needle, and possibly cassette deck. Put together, arranged in a particular way, the system works as a whole; we don't measure the individual components of the stereo system, we measure the system in terms of "sound," "quality," and "performance."

A screenplay is like a system; it is comprised of specific parts related and unified by action, character, and dramatic premise. We measure it, or evaluate it, in terms of how well it "works" or "doesn't work."

The screenplay, as "system," is made up of endings, beginnings, plot points, shots and effects, scenes, and sequences. Together, unified by the dramatic thrust of action and character, the story elements are "arranged" in a particular way and then revealed visually to create the totality known as "the screenplay." A story told with pictures.

As far as I'm concerned, the *sequence* is the most important element of the screenplay. It is the skeleton, or backbone, of your script; it holds everything together.

A SEQUENCE is *a series of scenes tied together, or connected, by one single idea.*

It is a unit, or block of dramatic action unified by *one single idea.* Remember the *chase* sequence in *Bullitt*? The *wedding* sequence that opened *The Godfather*? The *fight* sequence in *Rocky*? The *prom* sequence in *Carrie*? The *tennis* sequence in *Annie Hall* where Woody Allen meets Diane Keaton? The *UFO* sequence at the Devil's Tower in *Close Encounters of the Third Kind*? The *destruction of the Death Star* sequence from *Star Wars*?

A series of scenes connected by one single idea: a wedding, a funeral; a chase; a race; an election; a reunion; an arrival or departure; a coronation; a bank holdup. The sequence is a specific idea which can be expressed in a few words or less. The specific idea, like a "race"—the Indianapolis 500, for example—is a *unit*, or *block*, of *dramatic action* contained within the idea; it is the *context*, the space that holds the *content*, like an empty coffee cup. Once we establish the *context* of the sequence, we build it with *content*, or the specific details needed to create the sequence.

The sequence is the skeleton of the screenplay because it *holds* everything in place; you can literally "string," or "hang," a series of scenes together to create chunks of dramatic action.

You know those Chinese "block" games? You hold a large

block in your hand, release it, and a number of blocks flip-flop to the floor, all held by the block you hold in your hand.

That's what a sequence is like: a series of scenes connected by one single idea.

Every sequence has a definite beginning, middle, and end. Remember the football sequence from *M*A*S*H*? The teams arrive, put on their uniforms, warm up, growl at each other, and the coin is tossed. That's the beginning. They play the game. Back and forth they go; a play here, another there, a touchdown here, an injury there, and so on. After an exciting fourth quarter the game is finally over, the M*A*S*H team victorious, the opponents snarling in defeat. That's the middle of the sequence. The end comes when the game is over; they go to the locker rooms and change into their street clothes. That's the end of the "football sequence" in *M*A*S*H*.

A series of scenes tied together, or connected, by one single idea with a definite beginning, middle, and end. It is a microcosm of the screenplay, the same way a single cell contains the basic properties of the universe.

It's an important concept to understand in writing the screenplay. It is the organizational framework, the *form*, the *foundation*, the *blueprint* of your screenplay.

The contemporary screenplay, as practiced by such "modern" screenwriters as John Milius, Paul Schrader, Robert Towne, Stanley Kubrick, Steven Spielberg, to name a few, might be defined as *a series of sequences tied together, or connected, by the dramatic story line*. Milius's *Dillinger*, for example, is episodic in structure, as is Kubrick's *Barry Lyndon*, or Spielberg's *Close Encounters of the Third Kind*.

A sequence is a whole, a unit, a block of dramatic action, complete within itself.

Why is the sequence so important?

Look at the *paradigm*:

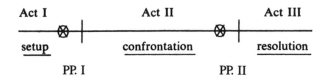

Before you can begin writing your screenplay, you need to know four things: the *opening*, the *plot point* at the end of Act I, the *plot point* at the end of Act II, and the *ending*. When you know what you're going to do in these specific areas, and you've done the necessary preparation on action and character, then you're ready to start writing. Not before.

Sometimes, but not always, these four story points are sequences, a series of scenes connected by one single idea; you might *open* your film with a *wedding* sequence as in *The Godfather*. You might use a sequence like Robert Redford discovering his *dead coworkers* in *Three Days of the Condor* as the plot point at the end of Act I. You might want to write a *party* sequence for the plot point at the end of Act II, as Paul Mazursky does in *An Unmarried Woman*, where Jill Clayburgh leaves with Alan Bates. You might use a *fight* sequence to end the film, as Sylvester Stallone does in *Rocky*.

Knowledge of the sequence is essential in writing a screenplay. Frank Pierson wrote *Dog Day Afternoon* with just 12 sequences. It should be noted that there are no specific number of sequences in a screenplay; you don't need 12, 18, or 20 sequences to make a screenplay. Your story will tell you how many sequences you need. Frank Pierson started off with four: opening, plot points at the end of Acts I and II, and ending. He added eight sequences and built that into a complete screenplay.

Think about it!

Suppose you want to open your film with a wedding sequence. Let's utilize the concept of *context* and *content*. The *context* is wedding. Let's create *content*.

Let's open on the day of the wedding. The bride wakes up in her house or apartment. The groom wakes up in his house or apartment. Perhaps they wake up together? Both prepare for the wedding. They dress, nervous and excited; the family hovers around; the photographer arrives, takes pictures; and they leave for the church or synagogue. That's the beginning of the sequence; it is comprised of five to eight individual scenes.

The middle is arriving at the church or synagogue (this could be a beginning as well), and the wedding ceremony itself. Friends and relatives arrive. The clergyman arrives. Bride and groom create their ceremony and when it's over, file out. An event always has a beginning, middle, and end. Think about it! The end is when they leave as a now-married couple; she throws the traditional bouquet and then they participate in the wedding reception. End it any way you want.

We started with the idea of *wedding*, the *context*, then created the *content*, and we'll end up with five to eight pages of a screenplay.

You can have as many or as few sequences as you want. There's no rule about the number you need. All you need to know is the *idea behind* the sequence, the *context*; and in order to create a series of scenes, the *content*.

Let's create a sequence; suppose we want to write a sequence about a "homecoming."

First, establish the *context*: suppose our character is returning home after several years in a POW camp in North Vietnam. He's on a plane with several other POWs.

He's going to be met by his family; father, mother, wife, or girlfriend. There's going to be military personnel at the airport, a military band, TV cameras and crew. Remember the first wave of POWs returning home?

Now, *content*. We need an opening for the sequence. Suppose we open on board the plane as it approaches San Francisco from Hawaii. Several military advisors are on board, preparing the POWs for their landing. They've been away for a long time. Things have changed. There's concern, anxiety, fear, apprehension, and relief as the POWs get ready.

We might "crosscut" between the plane and family getting up in the morning. ("Crosscutting" is a cinematic term for two events happening simultaneously; you "crosscut" or "intercut" between them. The opening of *Marathon Man* illustrates this technique. Edwin S. Porter began it in 1903 with *The Great Train Robbery*.)

As his family prepares to leave, they are quiet, tension high, expectation apparent; it's the moment they've been praying for. They leave the house and drive to the airport.

We intercut this with the POWs on the plane, spend time with our character. He's nervous, does not know what to expect.

The family arrives at the airport, parks the car. The military band plays, the personnel prepare to greet the POWs. The media set up their cameras and equipment. This is the end of the beginning portion of the "homecoming" sequence.

Then, the wait.

The plane lands, taxies to the deplaning area, stops. The doors slide open, the POWs depart amidst the blaring of military music. Home again.

You see how it's shaping up?

The reunion of family and friends is a dramatic moment in the sequence. The family embraces; father quiet, possibly with tears in his eyes, his mother laughing and crying as she tells her son how great he looks, even though he's 30 or 40 pounds underweight. The reunion is awkward and heartfelt. There may be some questions from the media.

They leave the airport. Our character searches out a few of his friends and they say their good-byes; he gets into the car with his family and leaves the airport.

Beginning, middle, and end, all connected by one single idea—"homecoming." It could be 10 to 12 pages long.

Remember the "party" sequence in *Midnight Cowboy*? Dustin Hoffman and Jon Voight decide to go to a party. They find the apartment, walk up the stairs, and enter. The party is in full swing, bizarre, unreal. They mingle, exchange words with several people, Jon Voight meets Brenda Vaccaro. Dustin Hoffman leaves, and Jon Voight goes home with Brenda Vaccaro.

Beginning, middle, and end.

In *All the President's Men*, written by William Goldman, from the book by Bernstein and Woodward, there is a sequence dealing with the "list of 100," the Committee to Re-Elect the President, known as CREEP. Deep Throat has told Robert Redford to "follow the money"; obtaining the CREEP list is the first step. Now what?

The sequence begins with Robert Redford and Dustin Hoffman pinpointing the identity of the people. Then, they find out where they live. They approach the people working for CREEP, but no one will talk to them, much less reveal anything. Scene after scene is built up dramatizing this until Woodward and Bernstein are about to call it quits.

That's when it happens. Hoffman meets a bookkeeper who

talks and now they have the information they're looking for; the amount of money in the slush fund, and the five people responsible for doling it out. The "CREEP" sequence is 15 pages long.

The "reservoir" sequence in *Chinatown* is another example. At the beginning of the second act, Jack Nicholson is looking for Mr. Mulwray. Faye Dunaway tells him he might be at the Oak Pass Reservoir, so Nicholson drives there.

At the beginning of the sequence, he arrives at the reservoir and is stopped by the policeman at the gate. He lies to the officer, and hands him a business card he lifted from the Department of Water and Power; he gains entrance and drives to the site of the reservoir.

In the middle of the sequence he arrives at the reservoir and sees an ambulance and rescue vehicle. He meets Lt. Escobar, the man he worked with in Chinatown when he was a cop. The two men don't like each other. Escobar asks Gittes what he's doing there and Nicholson replies he's looking for Mulwray. Escobar points and we see Mulwray's dead body being hauled up the water duct. As Morty, the coroner, says, "Ain't that something? Middle of a drought, and the water commissioner drowns—only in L.A."

A *sequence* is a series of scenes connected by one single idea, with a definite beginning, middle, and end.

What follows is the "I'm-as-mad-as-hell" sequence from *Network*, by Paddy Chayefsky. It is a perfect illustration of a sequence. Howard Beale, played by Peter Finch, has mysteriously disappeared from William Holden's apartment just before he's scheduled to go on the air. Frantically, Holden and other network executives try to locate him. It's raining out, and Finch has been wandering around in pajamas and raincoat. Note the construction of the sequence. It has a definite beginning, middle, and end. Notice how it builds, how Faye Dunaway, as Diana, expands the action dramatically and how it peaks with an emotional high.

(page 78 of screenplay)

EXT: UBS BUILDING—
SIXTH AVENUE—NIGHT—6:40 P.M.

THUNDER CRASHES—RAIN lashes the street. PEDESTRIANS struggle against the slashing rain. The streets gleam wetly, the heavy TRAFFIC heading uptown crushes and HONKS along, erratic enfilades of headlights in the shiny, black streets—

CLOSER ANGLE of entrance to UBS Building. HOWARD BEALE, wearing a coat over his pajamas, drenched to the skin, his mop of gray hair plastered in streaks to his brow, hunched against the rain, climbs the steps and pushes the glass door at the entrance and goes into—

INT: UBS BUILDING—LOBBY

TWO SECURITY GUARDS at the desk watch HOWARD pass—

> SECURITY GUARD
> How do you do, Mr. Beale?

HOWARD stops, turns, stares haggardly at the SECURITY GUARD.

> HOWARD
> *(mad as a loon)*
> I have to make my witness.

SECURITY GUARD
(an agreeable fellow)
Sure thing, Mr. Beale.

HOWARD plods off to the elevators.

INT: NETWORK NEWS CONTROL ROOM

Murmured, efficient activity as in previous scenes. DIANA
stands in the back in the shadows. On the SHOW MONITOR,
JACK SNOWDEN, BEALE's replacement, has been doing
the news straight—

SNOWDEN (on console)
. . . the Vice-President designate was on the
road today and stopped off in Provo, Utah, and,
in a speech in the basketball arena at Brigham
Young University—

PRODUCTION ASSISTANT
Five seconds—

(79)

TECHNICAL DIRECTOR
Twenty-five in Provo—

DIRECTOR
And . . . two—

SNOWDEN (on monitor)
Mr. Rockefeller had some strong words to say
about the Arab oil-producing nations. More on
that story from Edward Douglas—

All this is UNDER and OVERLAPPED by HARRY
HUNTER answering a BUZZ on his phone—

> HUNTER
> *(on phone)*
Yeah? . . . Okay—
> *(hangs up, to DIANA)*
He came in the building about five minutes ago.

> DIRECTOR
Get ready to roll her—

> PRODUCTION ASSISTANT
Ten seconds coming to one—

> DIANA
Tell Snowden if he comes in the studio to let him go on.

> HUNTER
> *(to the DIRECTOR)*
Did you get that, Gene?

The DIRECTOR nods, passes on the instructions to his A.D. on the studio floor. On the SHOW MONITOR, we are seeing footage of Rockefeller crowding his way to the speaker's rostrum, and we are hearing the VOICE of Edward Douglas in Provo, Utah—

> DOUGLAS
> *(on the phone)*
This was Rockefeller's first public appearance since he was named Vice-President designate, and he spoke sharply about inflation and high Arab oil prices—

On the SHOW MONITOR, Rockefeller flips onto the screen to say—

ROCKEFELLER (on monitor)
Perhaps the most dramatic evidence of the political impact on inflation is the action by the OPEC countries and the Arab oil countries in arbitrarily raising the price of oil four hundred percent—

Nobody in the control room is paying too much attention to Rockefeller; they are all watching the double bank of black-and-white monitors which show HOWARD BEALE entering the studio, drenched, hunched, staring gauntly off into his own space, moving with single-minded purpose across the studio floor past cameras and cables and nervous CAMERA-MEN, SOUND MEN, ELECTRICIANS, ASSISTANT DIRECTORS, and ASSOCIATE PRODUCERS, to his desk, which is being vacated for him by JACK SNOWDEN. On the SHOW MONITOR, the film clip on Rockefeller has come to an end.

DIRECTOR
And one—

—and, suddenly, the obsessed face of HOWARD BEALE, gaunt, haggard, red-eyed with unworldly fervor, hair streaked and plastered on his brow, manifestly mad, fills the MONITOR SCREEN.

HOWARD (on monitor)
I don't have to tell you things are bad. Everybody knows things are bad. It's a depression. Everybody's out of work or scared of losing their job, the dollar buys a nickel's worth, banks are going bust, shopkeepers keep a gun under the counter, punks are running wild in the

streets, and there's nobody anywhere who seems to know what to do, and there's no end to it. We know the air's unfit to breathe and our food is unfit to eat, and we sit and watch our tee-vees while some local newscaster tells us today we had fifteen homicides and sixty-three violent crimes, as if that's the way it's supposed to be. We all know things are bad. Worse than bad. They're crazy. It's like everything's going crazy. So we don't go out any more. We sit in the house, and slowly the world we live in gets smaller, and all we ask is, please, at least leave us alone in our own living rooms. Let me

(81)

have my toaster and my tee-vee and my hair dryer and my steel-belted radials, and I won't say anything, just leave us alone. Well, I'm not going to leave you alone. I want you to get mad—

ANOTHER ANGLE showing the rapt attention of the PEOPLE in the control room, especially of DIANA—

HOWARD *(contd.)*

I don't want you to riot. I don't want you to protest. I don't want you to write your congressmen. Because I wouldn't know what to tell you to write. I don't know what to do about the depression and the inflation and the defense budget and the Russians and crime in the street. All I know is first you got to get mad. You've got to say: "I'm mad as hell and I'm not going to take this any more. I'm a human being, goddammit. My life has value." So I want you to get up now.

I want you to get out of your chairs and go to the window. Right now. I want you to go to the window, open it, and stick your head out and yell. I want you to yell: "I'm mad as hell and I'm not going to take this any more!"

DIANA
(grabs HUNTER's shoulder)
How many stations does this go out live to?

HUNTER
Sixty-seven. I know it goes out to Atlanta and Louisville, I think—

HOWARD (on monitor)
Get up from your chairs. Go to the window. Open it. Stick your head out and yell and keep yelling—

But DIANA has already left the control room and is scurrying down—

INT: CORRIDOR
—yanking doors open, looking for a phone, which she finds in—

(82)

INT: AN OFFICE

DIANA
(seizing the phone)
Give me Stations Relations—
(the call goes through)
Herb, this is Diana Dickerson, are you watching? Because I want you to call every affiliate carrying this live— ... I'll be right up—

INT: ELEVATOR AREA—FIFTEENTH FLOOR

DIANA bursts out of the just-arrived elevator and strides down to where a clot of EXECUTIVES and OFFICE PERSONNEL are blocking an open doorway. DIANA pushes through to—

INT: THACKERAY'S OFFICE—
STATIONS RELATIONS

HERB THACKERAY on the phone, staring up at HOWARD BEALE on his wall monitor—

> HOWARD (on monitor)
> —First, you have to get mad. When you're mad enough—

Both THACKERAY's SECRETARY's office and his own office are filled with his STAFF. The Assistant VP Stations Relations, a 32-year-old fellow named RAY PITOFSKY, is at the SECRETARY's desk, also on the phone. Another ASSISTANT VP is standing behind him on the SECRETARY's other phone—

> DIANA
> *(shouting to THACKERAY)*
> Whom are you talking to?

> THACKERAY
> WCGG, Atlanta—

> DIANA
> Are they yelling in Atlanta, Herb?

> HOWARD (on console)
> —we'll figure out what to do about the depression—

                         THACKERAY
                         (on phone)
              Are they yelling in Atlanta, Ted?

INT: GENERAL MANAGER'S OFFICE—
AFFILIATE—ATLANTA

The GENERAL MANAGER of WCGG, Atlanta, a portly
                                                    (83)

58-year-old man, is standing by the open windows of his
office, staring out into the gathering dusk, holding his phone.
The station is located in an Atlanta suburb, but from far off
across the foliage surrounding the station, there can be heard
a faint RUMBLE. On his office console, HOWARD BEALE
is saying—

                      HOWARD (on console)
              —and the inflation and the oil crisis—

                      GENERAL MANAGER
                         (into phone)
              Herb, so help me, I think they're yelling—

INT: THACKERAY'S OFFICE

                         PITOFSKY
              (at SECRETARY'*s desk, on the phone)*
              They're yelling in Baton Rouge.

DIANA grabs the phone from him and listens to the people
of Baton Rouge yelling their anger in the streets—

                      HOWARD (on console)
              —Things have got to change. But you can't
              change unless you're mad. You have to get mad.
              Go to the window—

DIANA
*(gives phone back to PITOFSKY;
her eyes glow with excitement)*
The next time somebody asks you to explain
what ratings are, you tell them: that's ratings!
(exults)
Son of a bitch, we struck the mother lode!

INT: MAX'S APARTMENT—LIVING ROOM

MAX, MRS. SCHUMACHER, and their 17-year-old daughter, CAROLINE, watching the Network News Show—

HOWARD (on the set)
—Stick your head out and yell. I want you to
yell: "I'm mad as hell and I'm not going to take
this any more!"

(84)

CAROLINE gets up from her chair and heads for the living-room window.

LOUISE SCHUMACHER
Where are you going?

CAROLINE
I want to see if anybody's yelling.

HOWARD (on TV set)
Right now. Get up. Go to your window—

CAROLINE opens the window and looks out on the rain-swept streets of the upper East Side, the bulking, anonymous apartment houses and the occasional brownstones. It is thunder-dark; a distant clap of THUNDER CRASHES somewhere off and LIGHTNING shatters the dank darkness. In the sudden HUSH following the thunder, a thin voice down the block can be heard shouting:

>   THIN VOICES (*o.s.*)
>   I'm mad as hell and I'm not going to take this
>   any more!

>   HOWARD (on TV set)
>   —open your window—

MAX joins his daughter at the window. RAIN sprays his face—

MAX'S POV. He sees occasional windows open, and, just across from his apartment house, a MAN opens the front door of a brownstone—

>   MAN
>   *(shouts)*
>   I'm mad as hell and I'm not going to take this
>   any more!

OTHER SHOUTS are heard. From his twenty-third-floor vantage point, MAX sees the erratic landscape of Manhattan buildings for some blocks, and silhouetted HEADS in window after window, here, there, and then seemingly everywhere, SHOUTING out into the slashing black RAIN of the streets—

>   VOICES
>   I'm mad as hell and I'm not going to take this
>   any more!

A terrifying enormous CLAP of natural THUNDER, followed by a frantic brilliant FULGURATION of LIGHTNING; and now the gathering CHORUS of scattered

(85)

SHOUTS seems to be coming from the whole, huddled, black horde of the city's people, SCREAMING together in fury, an indistinguishable tidal roar of human rage as formidable as the natural THUNDER again ROARING, THUNDERING, RUMBLING above. It sounds like a Nuremberg rally, the air thick and trembling with it—

FULL SHOT of MAX, standing with his DAUGHTER by the open terrace window-doors, RAIN spraying against them, listening to the stupefying ROARS and THUNDERING rising from all around him. He closes his eyes, sighs, there's nothing he can do about it any more; it's out of his hands.

At the beginning, Howard Beale enters the UBS building, says hello to the guards, then prepares to "make my witness." He moves to the Network News Control Room.

The middle is the broadcast and speech, and over this, we see the reactions he's causing; everywhere, inside and outside, people are "mad as hell" and yelling out the windows.

The sequence ends as William Holden suddenly acknowledges the emotional power of Howard Beale. "There's nothing he can do about it any more; it's out of his hands."

It is a classic sequence—a complete unit of dramatic action; a series of scenes connected by one single idea with a beginning, middle, and end.

∗　　∗　　∗

As an exercise: Sketch out a sequence in your screenplay; find the idea, create the *context*, add *content*, then design it focusing on beginning, middle, and end. List four sequences you need to write in your screenplay; like the opening, plot points at the end of Acts I and II, and the ending. Design them.

9

The Plot Point

*Wherein we illustrate the concept and
nature of the plot point:*

When you're writing a screenplay, you have no objectivity at
all—no overview. You can't see anything except the scene
you're writing, the scene you've written, and the scene you're
going to write. Sometimes you can't even see that.

It's like climbing a mountain. When you're moving toward
the top, all you see is the rock directly in front of you, and
the one above you. Only when you reach the top can you
gaze at the panorama below.

The hardest thing about writing is knowing what to
write. When you're writing a screenplay you have to know
where you're going; you have to have a *direction*—a line of
development leading to the resolution, the ending.

If you don't you're in trouble. It's very easy to get lost
within the maze of your own creation.

That's why the *paradigm* is so important—it gives you
direction. Like a road map. On the road, through Arizona,
New Mexico, on through the vast reaches of Texas and
across the high plains of Oklahoma, you don't know where
you are, much less where you've been. All you can see is the
flat, barren landscape broken only by silver flashes from the
sun.

* 114

When you're *in* the *paradigm*, you can't *see* the *paradigm*. That's why the plot point is so important. The PLOT POINT is an incident, or event, that "hooks" into the action and spins it around into another direction.

It moves the story forward.

The plot points at the end of Acts I and II *hold* the *paradigm* in place. They are the anchors of your story line. Before you begin writing, you need to know four things: ending, beginning, plot point at the end of Act I, and plot point at the end of Act II.

Here's the *paradigm* again:

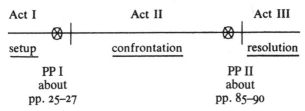

Throughout this book I stress the importance of the plot points at the end of Acts I and II. You must know the plot points at the end of each act before you begin writing. When your screenplay is completed, it may contain as many as 15 plot points. How many you have, again, depends upon your story. Each plot point *moves* the story *forward*, toward the resolution.

Chinatown is structured from plot point to plot point; each plot point carefully moves the action forward.

The script, as we've seen, opens with Gittes being hired by the phony Mrs. Mulwray to find out who her husband is having an affair with. Gittes follows Mulwray from council chambers to reservoir, later discovers him in the company of a young woman. He takes pictures, returns to the office, and, as far as he's concerned, the case is closed.

When he's getting a haircut he learns someone has released the story, along with pictures, to the newspaper.

Who did it? And why?

Gittes returns to his office and a young woman is waiting to see him. Has he ever seen her before? she asks. No. He would have remembered.

She tells him if he doesn't know her, then how could *she* hire him? *She* is Mrs. Evelyn Mulwray, the *real* Mrs. Mulwray (Faye Dunaway); since she did not hire him, she's going to sue him for libel and take away his detective license. She leaves.

Gittes is stunned. If that's the *real* Mrs. Mulwray, who hired him? And why? With the "love scandal" front-page news, he knows he's been set up—framed. Someone, he doesn't know who, wants him to take the "fall," and there's no way Jake Gittes is going to take a fall for anybody. His ass is on the line and he's going to find out who set him up. And why.

End of Act I.

What moment in that block of dramatic action "hooks" into the action and spins it around into another direction? Is it when the phony Mrs. Mulwray hires him? When the story is released to the newspaper? Or when the real Mrs. Mulwray shows up?

When Faye Dunaway enters the picture, the action shifts from a job completed to a possible libel suit and loss of his license. He'd better find out *who* set him up—then he'll find out *why*.

The *plot point* at the end of Act I is when the *real* Mrs. Mulwray shows up. That event spins the action around, shifts it into another direction. *Direction*, remember, is a line of development.

Act II opens with Nicholson driving up the long driveway

to the Mulwray house. Mr. Mulwray is not there. But Mrs. Mulwray is. They exchange a few words, and she tells him her husband might be at the Oak Pass Reservoir.

Nicholson goes to the Oak Pass Reservoir. There he meets Lt. Escobar (both were cops in Chinatown together; Nicholson left and Escobar made lieutenant) and learns Mulwray is dead, apparently as a result of an accident.

Mulwray's death presents another problem, or obstacle, for Gittes. In the *paradigm*, the dramatic *context* for Act II is *confrontation*.

Gittes' dramatic need is to find out *who* set him up, and *why*. So Robert Towne creates obstacles to that need. Mulwray is dead. Murdered, Gittes finds out later. Who did it? This is a plot point, but not *the* plot point at the end of Act I; it is simply a plot point within the structure of Act II. There are ten such plot points in the second act of *Chinatown*.

Mulwray's death is an incident or event that "hooks" into the action and spins it around into another direction. The story *moves forward*. Gittes is involved, whether he likes it or not.

Later, he receives a phone call from a mysterious "Ida Sessions," the woman, it turns out, who hired him in the beginning; the phony Mrs. Mulwray. She tells him to look in the obituary column of the paper for "one of those people," whatever that means. She hangs up. Soon after, she is found murdered, and Escobar is certain Nicholson is involved.

The theme of "water" has been introduced several times, and Gittes follows it. He goes to the Hall of Records and checks out the owners of land in the Northwest San Fernando Valley. He finds most of the land has been sold within the last few months. Remember the farmer's question on page 10: "Who's paying you [to steal the water from the Valley], Mr. Mulwray?"

When Gittes drives out to investigate an avocado grove, he is attacked by a farmer and his sons and beaten unconscious. They think he's the man who's been poisoning their water. When he regains consciousness, Faye Dunaway is there—called by the farmers.

Driving back to L.A., Nicholson discovers one of the names in the obituary column mentioned by Ida Sessions is cited as the owner of a large parcel of land in the Valley. Strange. He died at a place called the Mar Vista Home for the Aged.

Together, Gittes and Evelyn Mulwray drive to the Mar Vista old-age home. Gittes learns most of the new owners of land parcels in the Valley are living there, unaware of their purchase. It's phony—the whole thing's a scam. His suspicions confirmed, he's attacked by thugs, but Gittes and Evelyn manage to get away.

They drive back to her place.

These incidents or events are all plot points. They move the story forward.

At her house, Nicholson asks if she has any peroxide to clean his nose wound. She takes him into the bathroom, comments on the severity of the cut, daubs at the wound. He notices something in her eye, a slight color defect. He leans over and kisses her. It's a beautiful scene. They make love.

Finished, they lie in bed making small talk.

The phone rings. She looks at him; he looks at her. It continues ringing. Finally, she answers it, suddenly becomes agitated, hangs up. She tells Gittes he must leave. Immediately. She enjoyed the time spent together, but something important's come up and she has to leave.

Something's come up. What? Gittes wants to find out. He knocks the taillight out of her car and follows her to a house in the Echo Park section of Los Angeles.

End of Act II.

At this point in the story, we still don't know two things; (1) who was the girl Mulwray was with before he was murdered; and (2) who set up Nicholson, and why. Gittes knows the answers to both questions are related, though unresolved. **What's the plot point at the end of Act II?** When Gittes finds the glasses in the pool at Mulwray's house. That's the plot point at the end of Act II. "An incident, or event, that 'hooks' into the action and spins it around in another direction."

Act III is the *resolution* and what Nicholson learns resolves the story.

Gittes learns the girl is Dunaway's "daughter/sister," sired by her father (John Huston). It also answers the question why Faye Dunaway does not talk to her father, and why John Huston is after the girl. We also learn Huston is responsible for the three murders, as well as everything else; "either you bring the water to L.A., or you bring L.A. to the water," he says.

That's the dramatic "hook" of the movie. And it works, beautifully. The premise of money, power, and influence being a corruptive force is established; as Gittes tells Curly on page 3: "You gotta be rich to kill somebody, anybody, and get away with it." If you've got enough money and power, Towne seems to say, you can get away with anything —even murder.

When Faye Dunaway dies at the end of the film, John Huston spirits his daughter/granddaughter away and "gets away" with everything. Ironically, the incident that drove Gittes off the police-force beat in Chinatown has repeated itself: "I tried to help someone and all I ended up doing was hurting them," he had told Faye Dunaway earlier.

Full circle, turn. Gittes can't deal with it. He has to be restrained by his two partners; the last words of the script are: "Forget it, Jake—it's Chinatown."

Do you see how the plot points at the end of Acts I and II "hook" into the action and spin it around into another direction? They move the story forward, to its resolution.

Chinatown moves to its conclusion, step by step, scene by scene, plot point by plot point. There are ten such plot points in Act II, two in Act III.

The next time you go to a movie see if you can locate the plot points at the end of Act I and Act II. Every film you see will have definite plot points. All you have to do is find them. About 25 minutes into the film an incident or event will occur. Discover *what* it is, *when* it occurs. It might be difficult at first, but the more you do it the easier it gets. Check your watch.

Do the same for Act II. Just check your watch about 85 to 90 minutes into the film. It's an excellent exercise.

Let's take a look at the plot points in: *Three Days of the Condor, Rocky, Network, Nashville, An Unmarried Woman,* and *Close Encounters of the Third Kind.*

Here's the *paradigm*:

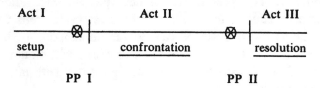

We're looking for the plot points at the end of Acts I and II.

In *Three Days of the Condor*, Robert Redford works at "The American Literary Historical Society," a "reading" cell of the CIA. The employees read books. When the film opens, Redford arrives at work, late, and goes about his office routine. He's sent out to get lunch for the staff, and when he returns, everyone's dead, brutally murdered.

Who did it? Why?

Redford doesn't have time to think. He should be dead, too—only because he was "out to lunch" is he still living. It takes him a while to grasp the situation; when he does, he knows someone is going to kill him. He doesn't know who and he doesn't know why—all he knows is that he's going to be killed.

End of Act I.

Lorenzo Semple, Jr., and David Rayfiel, the screenwriters, set up the story the following way: Act I establishes that Redford has uncovered some kind of conspiracy developing within the CIA. He doesn't know *what* it is; all he knows is that his friends and coworkers are dead.

And he's next on the list.

The plot point at the end of Act I is when he *returns* from lunch and discovers everybody dead. It is Redford's *reaction* to this "incident/event" that spins the action around in another direction.

In Act II the dramatic context is *confrontation*. Redford encounters obstacles everywhere. His best friend—also in the CIA—is sent to meet him but is killed, and his death is blamed on Redford. Out of dramatic necessity (you can't have the main character talking to himself—monologues don't work!) he kidnaps Faye Dunaway. Redford is a *victim* all the way through the second act; he spends the next 60 minutes (60 pages) being hunted down by the hired assassin (Max von Sydow). He constantly reacts to this situation.

When he's attacked in Faye Dunaway's apartment by the mailman killer, he's got to *do* something. He's got to turn the situation around; from being a victim, to being the attacker, the aggressor, in the situation.

Have you ever been a victim? We all have at one time or another. It's no fun. You've got to get "on top" of the situation, and not be run by it. Redford does turn it around, and

Faye Dunaway helps him do it. She enters the CIA headquarters, pretending to apply for a job. She "accidentally" blunders into Cliff Robertson's office, the man in charge of the "Condor affair," sees what he looks like—Redford has never seen him before—apologizes, and leaves. Over lunch at a restaurant, Redford and Dunaway abduct Cliff Robertson. Redford questions him intently and tells the CIA man the information that will ultimately lead to his discovery of what's really going on—there is a CIA within the CIA.

The plot point at the end of Act II is when Redford turns the action around—from being a victim to being the attacker, from being hunted to being the hunter. By abducting Cliff Robertson, Redford "spins the action around into another direction."

In Act III Redford follows his lead to the man responsible for the scheme—Lionel Atwell. Redford confronts Atwell at his house, finds he has set up a CIA within the CIA and is the man behind the deaths of the others. The reason—oil fields. Max von Sydow enters, abruptly kills the high-ranking CIA official, and spares Redford. At least for now. The assassin is back in the employ of "the company," the CIA.

When you are writing your screenplay, the plot points become signposts, holding the story together and moving it forward.

Are there any exceptions to this rule? Do all movies have plot points? Maybe you can think of some that don't?

What about *Nashville*? Is that an exception?

Let's take a look. First, who's the main character of the film? Lily Tomlin? Ronee Blakeley? Ned Beatty? Keith Carradine?

I had the opportunity to hear Joan Tewkesbury, the screenwriter, talk at Sherwood Oaks about writing *Nashville*.

She spoke about the difficulty of writing several characters at once, and how she had to find some kind of unifying theme in the film to hold it together. She went to Nashville twice to do research before writing the film—both times for several weeks. She realized the main character of the film—that is, who the movie is about—is the city of Nashville. *It* is the main character. When she said that, I suddenly realized the *plot point is a function of the main character.* Follow the main character in a story and you'll find the plot points at the end of Acts I and II.

Nashville is the main character because it holds everything together, like a *context*; everything occurs within the city. There are several major characters in the film and they all move the action forward.

The film opens at Nashville Airport as the major characters arrive. We are introduced to them, catch glimpses of their characters and personalities, their hopes and dreams. After Ronee Blakeley arrives, they leave the airport simultaneously but in separate cars, and like Keystone Kops bumble into each other in the snafu of a freeway traffic jam.

The plot point at the end of Act I is when they leave the airport. The action shifts direction, from airport to freeway, and allows the action of the story to *move forward* as needed by the characters.

Act II details their characters and interactions; the dramatic need of each character is established, the conflicts generated, courses plotted. At the end of the second act, Michael Murphy, the political front man, convinces Allan Garfield to let Ronee Blakeley sing at the political rally.

That's the plot point at the end of Act II. It is the "incident, or event, that spins the story around" and takes us into Act III and the resolution.

Act I takes place at the airport; Act II in various locations; Act III at the Parthenon, just outside Nashville. We follow the main characters as they arrive at the Parthenon. The rally begins, ends with the assassination attempt that seriously wounds or kills Ronee Blakeley.

In that final flurry of action, as the throng of people react fearfully, Barbara Harris takes the microphone and leads everyone in song. Together, they sing in harmony as sirens screech and panic reigns. Nashville, after all, *is* a city of music.

Robert Altman, the director, is a master craftsman of dramatic structure; his films may look randomly composed but in reality they are executed with sculpted finesse. *Nashville* fits the *paradigm* to a tee.

What about *Network*? Is that an exception? No. It follows the *paradigm* perfectly. Most people get hung up in trying to decide *who* the main character is. Who is the main character? William Holden? Faye Dunaway? Peter Finch? Robert Duvall?

No. The "network" is the main character. It feeds everything, like a system; the people are parts of the whole, replaceable parts, at that. Network continues on, indestructible; people come and go. Just like life.

In the same way that Nashville is the main character, so is Network the main character. If you grasp this, everything follows naturally.

When the film opens, a narrator states that this story is about Howard Beale (Peter Finch), and we find William Holden and Finch getting drunk in a bar. The best of friends, Holden is head of the news department and must fire newscaster Finch after 15 years because of poor ratings. When Finch goes on the air and states he's being replaced, "a victim of the ratings," he makes the dramatic pronouncement he's going to kill himself on the air!

It becomes a front-page story and creates havoc. The ratings go up. The network, in the form of executive Robert

Duvall, is paranoid about Finch's statement; Duvall wants him off the air immediately.

But Faye Dunaway, as director of programming, sees a unique opportunity. She convinces Robert Duvall to put Finch back on the air as a kind of mad prophet who's had it with the "bullshit" we bitterly call a "life-style" or "standard of living."

Finch goes back on the air. The ratings improve and soon Howard Beale's is the number-one show on TV. Then, he oversteps himself and exposes the pending acquisition of the network by Saudi Arabian investors.

Finch is hauled "on the carpet" by the president of the corporate network, CCA; Ned Beatty, in a magnificent scene, raves that Peter Finch has "tampered with the natural order of things"; the Arabs took a lot of money out of this country, he tells Finch, and now they have to put it back in. It's a natural flow, like gravity, or the ocean tides.

Ned Beatty convinces Peter Finch to spread the gospel as seen by the president of CCA—the individual is dead, but the corporation lives! The people don't buy it; Finch's ratings drop. As in the beginning, Network wants to get Finch off the air, but Ned Beatty, the president, refuses. Robert Duvall, Faye Dunaway, and the others have a problem. How do they get Finch off the air? The film ends with Peter Finch being assassinated on the air—in a variation on what he had threatened at the beginning of the film. Endings and beginnings, right?

What are the plot points at the end of Acts I and II?

Howard Beale is going to be fired, but gets another chance when Faye Dunaway convinces Robert Duvall to put him back on the air. That's the plot point at the end of Act I. It occurs 25 minutes into the film. It "hooks" into the action and spins it around. Because of Faye Dunaway, Peter Finch has a top-rated show until he oversteps himself with the "takeover speech." That speech is the plot point at the end of Act II.

That "incident" results in Ned Beatty telling Peter Finch to change his message and spread the gospel according to Beatty. This leads to the resolution; Finch must be taken off the air because of poor ratings, and the only way to do that is to kill him. And they do it. It is biting satire and very funny.

Knowledge of the plot point is an essential requirement in writing a screenplay. Be aware of plot points, look for them in the films you see, discuss them in the scripts you read.

Every film has them.

What about the plot points in *Rocky*? In Act I, Rocky is a down-and-out fighter who "wants to be someone"; in reality, he's a "bum" who picks up some odd dollars as the muscle for a childhood friend.

By coincidence, Rocky gets the opportunity to fight the Heavyweight Champion of the World. Is that a plot point or is that a plot point! It occurs about 25 minutes into the film.

Rocky overcomes the barriers of laziness and inertia, forces himself into shape, knowing all the time he can't win. Apollo Creed is just too good. If he can stay on his feet for 15 rounds with the world's champion, however, it becomes a personal victory. And that becomes his "goal," his dramatic "need"—we could all take a lesson from Rocky.

The plot point at the end of Act II is when Rocky races up the steps of the museum and dances around in victory to the tune of "Gonna Fly, Now." As the script reads, he's as ready as he'll ever be to fight Apollo Creed. He's done all he can— whatever's going to happen is going to happen.

Act III is the fight sequence. It has a definite beginning, middle, and end, and Rocky, with inspiring strength and courage, fights Apollo Creed for 15 rounds. It is a personal victory.

When you see the movie you'll find Rocky selected to fight

Apollo Creed approximately 25 minutes into the film; Rocky is "ready" to fight about 88 minutes in. The rest of the movie is the fight.

Check it out!

An Unmarried Woman is another example. Act I, the setup, dramatizes the *married* life of Jill Clayburgh and Michael Murphy. Everything *seems* fine in their relationship, but if you look closely you can clearly see the strain on her husband. About 25 minutes into the film, Michael Murphy suddenly announces to Jill Clayburgh that he's in love with another woman; that he wants to live with her, possibly marry her. He wants out of the marriage.

Is that a plot point?

The second act deals with Jill Clayburgh's attempts to adjust to her new situation; formerly a married woman, she is now an unmarried woman, and a single parent.

Then she meets and has a one-night stand with artist Alan Bates. He wants to see her again; she refuses. She's getting used to the idea of being single. Shortly after they've had sex together, they meet again, at a party.

At the party, Bates scuffles with another artist over Clayburgh, and the two of them leave together. They like each other and decide to see each other again; it's not long before they create a relationship.

The party occurs 85 minutes into the film. Is that a plot point? Of course. Act I deals with the situation of "the marriage," Act II with Jill Clayburgh's adjustments to being "unmarried," and Act III with being "single" and forging a relationship with Alan Bates and a new sense of identity.

When you see a movie, determine the plot points. See whether the *paradigm* works or not.

As a form, the screenplay is constantly changing. A new generation of screenwriters, raised on TV—pictures, not words—are redefining and expanding the art of the screenplay. What works in terms of style and execution today may not work tomorrow.

Historically, of course, there have always been significant changes in the American film. From the romantic comedies and social dramas of the '30s, to the war movies and romantic detective stories of the '40s, to the fantasy fluff of the '50s, the violence of the '60s, and the political coverups and expansion of the woman's consciousness in the '70s, American movies have consistently evolved in terms of form and content.

From the early '60s—the time of *Hud* and *The Hustler*, two films, I think, that most heavily influenced the contemporary screenplay by refining the dramatic structure into three independent act divisions—the screenplay has become leaner, tighter, and more visual in style and execution.

At present, Hollywood is in a period of transition. Studios are experimenting with new sound systems, new equipment, and new visual techniques, devices that will force the filmmaker to expand and improve his craft. Film, like any living art form, evolves, a fusion of scientific advancement and artistic achievement.

There are two editions of Steven Spielberg's *Close Encounters:* the first edition, his original cut to meet the studio deadline, and then his recutting of the film, made a few years after the original release. As far as I'm concerned, the original *Close Encounters* is a film of the future. In terms of style, form, and execution, it transforms the structure of film and shows us tomorrow, today.

Take a look at the *paradigm*:

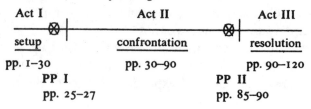

Approximately twenty-five minutes into the film Richard Dreyfuss is sitting in his truck when the power goes out and he is jolted from his seat. It is a wonderful and unusual event: Plot Point I. About eighty-eight minutes into the film, Dreyfuss reaches the Devil's Tower and manages to make his way inside the protected area. Plot Point II. Act III is his experience with the UFO.

This is the structure of Spielberg's recut version of the film. But the first edition is different: The original edition of the film is leaner, more visual, more episodic in form and structure. The advertising for the movie states that a "Close Encounter" of the First Kind is the visual *sighting* of a UFO; of the Second Kind is *physical evidence* of a UFO; and a "Close Encounter" of the Third Kind is *contact*.

Sighting, physical evidence, and contact. The film visually dramatizes these concepts; Act I is the visual *sighting* of the UFOs, Act II is the *physical evidence*, and Act III is *contact*.

Here's the *paradigm* for *Close Encounters:*

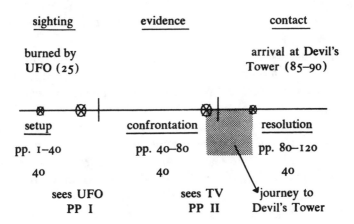

Act I is 40 pages, Act II is 40 pages, and Act III is 40 pages. (In reality, the film is 135 minutes, most of it in the form of additional action happening on the journey between the plot point at the end of Act II and the beginning of Act III.)

Twenty-five minutes into the film, Richard Dreyfuss is sitting in his truck at the railroad crossing, and is suddenly exposed to the blinding lights of a UFO; the experience is so intense he's literally "blown out" of his seat. This corresponds to the plot point at the end of Act I.

He's inexplicably "drawn" to a wooded hillside highway, and watches a group of UFOs streaking through the night sky. One man holds a sign; "stop and be friendly." It's a nice touch. He tries to convince his wife (Teri Garr) of the reality of his experience, but she doesn't believe him. Nobody believes him. He goes back to the hill, and waits. When the lights come, army helicopters swoop out of the sky. That's the end of Act I, *sighting*; it comes about 42 minutes into the film.

Act II deals with that *physical evidence*; at the end of Act I, Richard Dreyfuss is standing with Melinda Dillon, and we see her child (Cary Guffey) building an image of the mysterious mountain that comes to haunt them throughout the second act.

The act opens with Dreyfuss stuffing his pillow into the shape of a mountain; soon he becomes obsessed with it; numbers are received from the UFO and are analyzed as being the geographic coordinates of the Devil's Tower in Wyoming. When Dreyfuss *sees* the mountain on TV (while constructing the very same mountain in his living room) it is the plot point at the end of Act II. It occurs approximately 75 to 80 minutes into the film. That's where he must go.

He leaves wife and family behind, overcomes obstacle after obstacle, and finally reaches the Devil's Tower. This corresponds to the plot point on pages 85–90 at the end of Act II. Dreyfuss and Melinda Dillon are "captured" by the army units, but manage to break away and race toward the mysterious mountain. The resolution begins.

Act III, *contact,* shows Richard Dreyfuss and Melinda Dillon climbing the mountain to their appointed rendezvous. They edge down to the landing site, and like a stage in evolution where nature "selects" the surviving organism, Richard Dreyfuss goes on alone. In the splendor and wonder of some of the most magnificent special effects ever conceived (by Douglas Trumbull) earthling and alien greet each other and communicate spiritually through the universal language of music. Music, indeed, is the Seventh Wonder.

Within the structure of *Close Encounters* the paradigm holds, but is shifted to create a complete 40-minute unit, or block, of dramatic action contained within the cinematic context: Act I, *sighting*; Act II, *physical evidence*; and Act III, *contact.* I think this structure might be prevalent in the near future, as practiced by young filmmakers now in grade school.

The *form* is the future.

Knowledge and mastery of the plot point are an essential requirement of writing a screenplay. The plot points at the end of each act are the anchoring pins of dramatic action; they hold everything together. They are the signposts, goals, objectives, or destination points of each act—forged links in the chain of dramatic action.

*   *   *

As an exercise: Go to a film and find the plot points at the end of Acts I and II. Look at your watch. Time them. See whether the *paradigm* works. If you can't find them, look again. They're there.

Do you know the plot points at the end of Acts I and II in your screenplay?

10

The Scene

Wherein we approach the scene:

The scene is the single most important element in your screenplay. It is where something happens—where something *specific* happens. It is a specific unit of action—and the place you tell your story.

Good scenes make good movies. When you think of a good movie, you remember *scenes*, not the entire film. Think of *Psycho*. What scene do you recall? The shower scene, of course. What about *Butch Cassidy and the Sundance Kid*? *Star Wars*? *Citizen Kane*? *Casablanca*?

The way you present your scenes on the page ultimately affects the entire screenplay. A screenplay is a reading experience.

The purpose of the scene is to *move the story forward*.

A scene is as long or short as you want. It can be a three-page dialogue scene, or as short as a single shot—a car streaking down the highway. The scene is what you want it to be.

The story determines how long or how short your scene is. There is only one rule to follow; trust your story. It will tell you everything you need to know. I've noticed many people have a tendency to make a rule for everything. If there are 18 scenes and two sequences in the first 30 pages of some screenplay or movie, they feel *their* first 30 pages must have 18 scenes and two sequences. You can't write a screenplay following numbers as you do a drugstore painting.

It doesn't work—trust your story to tell you what you need to know.

We're going to approach the scene from two sides: We're going to explore the *generalities* of the scene, that is, the *form*, and then we'll examine the *specifics* of the scene; how you create a scene from the elements, or components you have within that scene.

Two things are in every scene—PLACE and TIME.

Where does your scene take *place*? In an office? A car? At the beach? In the mountains? On a crowded city street? What is the *location* of the scene?

The other element is *time*. What time of day or night does your scene take place? In the morning? Afternoon? Late at night?

Every scene occurs within a specific *place* at a specific *time*. All you need to indicate, however, is DAY or NIGHT.

Where does your scene take place? *Inside* or *outside*; or INT. for interior, EXT. for exterior. So the form of the scene becomes:

INT. LIVING ROOM—NIGHT
or
EXT. STREET—DAY

PLACE and TIME. You need to know these two things before you can build and construct a scene.

If you change either *place* or *time* it becomes a new scene.

We saw, in the first ten pages of *Chinatown*, Curly in

Jake's office, upset because of his wife. Gittes gives him a drink of cheap whiskey, they walk out of his office into the reception area.

When they move from Nicholson's office into the reception area, it is a new scene; they have changed *place*.

Gittes is called into his associate's office and hired by the phony Mrs. Mulwray. The scene in the associate's office is a new scene. They have changed the *place* of the scene—one scene in Gittes' office, another in the reception area, and another in his associate's office. Three scenes in the *office sequence*.

If your scene takes place in a house, and you move from the bedroom to kitchen to living room, you have three individual scenes. Your scene might take place in the bedroom between a man and woman. They kiss passionately, then move to the bed. When the CAMERA PANS to the window where the sky changes from night to day, then PANS back to our couple waking up, it is a new scene. You have changed the *time* of your scene.

If your character is driving a car up a mountain road at night and you want to show him at different locations, you must change your scenes accordingly: EXT. MOUNTAIN ROAD—NIGHT to EXT. MOUNTAIN ROAD, FURTHER—NIGHT.

There's a reason for this; the physical necessity of changing the position of the CAMERA for each scene or shot in the new location. Each scene requires a change in CAMERA position (Note: the word CAMERA is always capitalized in the screenplay) and therefore requires a change in lighting. That's why movie crews are so large and the cost of filming a movie is so expensive, approximately $10,000 per minute. As the price of labor escalates, the cost per minute increases and we end up paying more at the box office.

Scene changes are absolutely essential in the development of your screenplay. The scene is where it all happens—where you tell your story in *moving pictures.*

A scene is constructed in terms of beginning, middle, and end, just like a screenplay. Or, it can be presented in part, a portion of the whole like showing only the end of the scene. Again, there's no rule—it is your story, so you make the rules.

Every scene reveals at least one element of necessary story information to reader or audience. Very rarely does it provide more. The information the audience receives is the nucleus, or purpose, of the scene.

Generally, there are two kinds of scenes: one, where something happens *visually,* like an action scene—the chase that opens *Star Wars,* or the fight scenes in *Rocky.* The other is a *dialogue* scene between one or more persons. Most scenes combine the two. In a dialogue scene, there's usually some action going on, and in an action scene, there's usually some dialogue. A dialogue scene is usually about three pages long or less. That's three minutes of screen time. Sometimes it's longer, but not often. The "aborted" love scene in *Silver Streak* is nine pages long; a few scenes in *Network* are seven pages long. If you write a dialogue scene between two people, try to keep it under three pages. There's no room in your screenplay to be "cute," "clever," or "gimmicky." You can tell your life story in three minutes if you have to; most scenes in contemporary screenplays are only a few pages long.

Within the body of your scene, something specific happens —your *characters* move from point A to point B; or your *story* moves from point A to point B. Your story always moves forward. Even in "flashback." *Julia, Annie Hall,* and *Midnight Cowboy* are structured to include the flashback as an integral part of the story. The flashback is a technique used to expand the audience's comprehension of story, characters, and situation. It is also a dated technique in many ways. Tony Bill, the producer/director/actor, says, "When I see a flashback in a script, I know the story's in trouble. It's an easy way out for the novice writer." Your story should be executed in action, not flashback. Unless you're really creative, like Woody Allen in *Annie Hall*, or Alvin Sargent in *Julia*, avoid them.

They "date" your material immediately.

How do you go about creating a scene?

First create the *context*, then determine *content*.

What happens in the scene? What is the *purpose* of the scene? Why is it there? How does it move the story forward? What happens?

An actor sometimes approaches a scene by finding out what he's doing there, where he's been and where he's going after the scene. What is his purpose in the scene? Why is he there?

As writer, it's your responsibility to know why your characters are in a scene, and how their actions, or dialogue, move the story forward. You've got to know what happens to your characters *in* the scenes, as well as what happens to them *in between* the scenes; what happened between the office Monday afternoon, and Thursday evening at dinner? If you don't know, who does?

By creating *context*, you determine dramatic purpose and can build your scene line by line, action by action. By creating *context*, you establish *content*.

Okay. How do you do that?

First, find the *components* or *elements* within the scene. What aspect of your character's *professional* life, *personal* life, or *private* life is going to be revealed?

Let's go back to the story of three guys holding up the Chase Manhattan Bank. Suppose we want to write a scene where our characters definitely decide to rob the bank. Up until now, they've only talked about it. Now, they're going to do it. That's *context*. Now, *content*.

Where does your scene take place?

In the bank? Home? Bar? Inside a car? Walking in the park? The obvious place to set it would be in a quiet, secluded location, perhaps a rented car on the highway. That's the obvious place for the scene. It works, but maybe there's something more visual we can use; this is, after all, a movie.

Actors often play "against the grain" of a scene; that is, they approach the scene not from the obvious approach, but the *unobvious* approach. For example, they'll play an "angry" scene smiling softly, hiding their rage or anger beneath a façade of niceness. Brando is a master at this.

In *Silver Streak*, Colin Higgins writes a love scene between Jill Clayburgh and Gene Wilder in which they talk about flowers! It's beautiful. Orson Welles, in *The Lady from Shanghai*, had a love scene with Rita Hayworth in an aquarium, in front of the sharks and barracudas.

When you're writing a scene, look for a way that dramatizes the scene "against the grain."

Suppose we use a crowded pool hall, at night, as the setting for the "decision" scene in our Chase Manhattan Bank story. We can introduce an element of suspense in the scene; as our characters shoot pool and discuss their decision to rob the bank, a policeman enters, wanders around. It adds a touch of dramatic tension. Hitchcock does it all the time. Visually, we might open with a shot of the eight ball, then pull back to reveal our characters leaning over the table talking about the job.

Once the *context* is determined—the purpose, place, and time—then the *content* follows.

Suppose we want to write a scene about the ending of a relationship. How would we do it?

First—establish the purpose of the scene. In this case it is the ending of a relationship. Second—find out *where* the scene takes place and *when,* day or night. It could take place in a car, on a walk, in a movie theater, or a restaurant. Let's use a restaurant; it's an ideal place to end a relationship.

Here's *context.* Have they been together long? How long? In relationships about to end, usually one person wants it to end and the other person hopes it won't. Let's say *he* wants to end it with *her.* He doesn't want to hurt her; he wants to be as "nice" and "civilized" as he can.

Of course, it always backfires. Remember the breakup scene in *An Unmarried Woman,* where Michael Murphy has lunch with Jill Clayburgh, but can't force himself to say the words. He waits until they're on the street, after lunch, then breaks down and blurts out the words.

First, find the components of the scene. What is there in a restaurant that we can use dramatically? The waiters, the food, someone sitting nearby; an old friend?

The *content* of the scene now becomes part of the *context.*

He doesn't want to "hurt" her, so he's quiet and uncomfortable. Use the *uncomfortableness*: run-on sentences, staring off into the distance, watching nearby diners; perhaps the waiter overhears a few remarks, and he's a surly Frenchman, possibly gay. You get to choose!

This is a method that allows you to stay on top of your story, so the story's not on top of you. As a writer, you must exercise *choice* and *responsibility* in the construction and presentation of your scenes.

Look for conflicts; make something difficult, more difficult. It adds tension.

Remember the scene at the outdoor restaurant in *Annie Hall*? Annie tells Woody Allen that she just wants to be his "friend," and not continue their relationship. Both are uncomfortable and this adds tension to the scene by heightening the comedic overtones; when he leaves the restaurant he collides with several cars, tears up his driver's license in front of a policeman. It's hysterical! Woody Allen utilizes the situation for maximum dramatic effectiveness.

Comedy works by creating a situation, then letting people act and react to the situation and each other. In comedy, you can't have your characters playing for laughs; they have to believe what they're doing, otherwise it becomes forced and contrived, and therefore, unfunny.

Remember the Italian film *Divorce, Italian Style*, with Marcello Mastroianni? A classic film comedy, only a thin line separates it from being a classic tragedy. Comedy and tragedy are two sides of the same coin. Mastroianni is married to a woman who makes enormous sexual demands on him and he can't cope with it. Especially when he meets a voluptuous young cousin who's crazy about him. He wants a divorce but, alas, the Church won't recognize it. What's an Italian man to do? The only way the Church will recognize the end of the marriage is for the wife to die. But she's as healthy as a horse.

He decides to kill her. Under Italian law, the only way he can kill her with honor and get away with it is if she's unfaithful; he has to be cuckolded. So he sets out to find a lover for his wife.

That's the situation!

After many, many funny moments, she *is* unfaithful to him, and his Italian honor demands he take action. He tracks her and her lover to an island in the Aegean Sea, and searches for them, gun in hand.

The characters are caught within the web of circumstances

and play their roles with exaggerated seriousness; the result is film comedy at its best.

Woody Allen generates beautiful situations. In *Annie Hall, Sleeper,* and *Play It Again, Sam,* he creates a situation and then lets his characters react to it. In comedy, says Woody Allen, "acting funny is the worst thing you can do."

Comedy, like drama, depends on "real people in real situations."

Neil Simon creates marvelous people who operate at cross-purposes, then lets the "sparks fly" as they encounter obstacle after obstacle. He establishes a strong situation, then puts strong, believable people in it. In *The Goodbye Girl,* Richard Dreyfuss sublets an apartment from a friend, and when he arrives to take possession, in the midst of a driving rainstorm at three o'clock in the morning, he finds the apartment occupied by Marsha Mason and her daughter. She refuses to leave because "possession is nine-tenths of the law!"

What follows is scene after scene of verbal humor; they hate each other, tolerate each other, finally love each other.

When you set out to write a scene, find the purpose of the scene, then root it in place and time. Then find the elements or components within the scene to build it and make it work.

One of my favorite scenes from *Chinatown* is when Jack Nicholson and Faye Dunaway are at her house after the Mar Vista Home for the Aged sequence. During the previous 18 hours, Gittes has almost drowned, been beaten up twice, had his nose sliced, lost one Florsheim shoe, and has had no sleep at all. He's tired and hurts all over.

His nose hurts. He asks her if she has any peroxide to clean his nose wound, and she takes him into the bathroom. She daubs his nose, and he notices something in her eye, a slight color defect. Their eyes hold, then he leans forward and kisses her.

The next scene takes place after they've made love. It's a beautiful illustration of what you should look for when you plan a scene. Find the *components* within the scene to make it work; in this case, it was the hydrogen peroxide in the bathroom.

Every scene, like a sequence, an act, or an entire screenplay, has a definite beginning, middle, and end. But you only need to show *part* of the scene. You can choose to show only the beginning, just the middle, or only the end.

For example, in three-guys-holding-up-the-Chase-Manhattan-Bank, you can start the scene in the *middle* when they're playing pool. The beginning of the scene, where they arrive, get a table, practice, then start the game, does not have to be shown unless you choose to show it. The ending of the scene, when they leave the pool hall, doesn't have to be shown either.

Very rarely is a scene depicted in its entirety. The scene, more often than not, is a fragment of the *whole*. William Goldman, who wrote *Butch Cassidy and the Sundance Kid* and *All the President's Men,* among others, once remarked that he doesn't enter his scenes until the last possible moment; that is, just before the ending of some specific action in the scene.

In the bathroom scene in *Chinatown,* Towne shows the *beginning* of the love scene, then cuts to the *ending* of the bed scene.

You, as writer, are completely in control of how you create your scenes to move your story forward. You *choose* what part of the scene you are going to show.

Colin Higgins is a writer of unique film comedies. (With *Foul Play* he's become a director as well.) *Harold and Maude* is a fantastic comic situation—a young man of twenty and a woman of eighty create a special relationship together. *Har-*

old and Maude is a case where the audience gradually found the film and over a period of years made it an underground "classic" of the American cinema.

In *Silver Streak* Higgins creates a marvelous love scene that is "against the grain." Gene Wilder, as George, and Jill Clayburgh, as Hilly, have met in the dining car, like each other, and get drunk together. They decide to spend the evening together. She gets the room, and he gets the champagne. The scene opens as George returns to his compartment, flushed with alcohol and expectation.

(page 19 of screenplay)

INT. THE CORRIDOR—NIGHT

Giggling to himself and humming "The Atchison, Topeka and the Santa Fe," George makes his way down the corridor. Suddenly one of the Fat Men steps out of his compartment at the far end and begins walking toward George. George stops and leans against a door to let him pass. It is a very tight and difficult maneuver for the Fat Man to pass and in the struggle George's hand lands on the door handle. Immediately the door flies open and George staggers back into the room. He turns to see a large, ugly MEXICAN LADY in her nightshirt kneeling at her bed saying her prayers. She takes one look at George and in violent Spanish begins panic-praying to ward off the oncoming rape.

George freaks, and bowing and mumbling apologies, hurriedly exits to the safety of the corridor, closing the door behind him. He pauses for a moment to regain his composure, burps, and then starts off again. Immediately the second Fat

Man exits from his compartment and makes his way toward George. George sighs but not wishing to go through the whole scene again he backs up past the Mexican Lady's door, and knocks on the next door down. He opens it, steps inside for a second to let the Fat Man pass, then turns to the occupant. He is a very distinguished gentleman, suavely attired, who looks up from the papers he has been reading. This is ROGER DEVEREAU.

GEORGE

Excuse me.

Not waiting for a response George smiles and quickly closes the door. He continues on down the corridor.

INT. GEORGE'S CORRIDOR

George arrives outside his door and knocks.

HILLY'S VOICE

Come in.

George enters.

INT. GEORGE'S COMPARTMENT

True to her word Hilly has gotten the porter to push back the partition and make their two rooms into one. The effect is remarkably spacious—and very romantic as the two couches have been turned into beds. George looks around and smiles.

GEORGE

This is *very nice.*

Hilly is lying on her bed with her shoes on. She is putting a tape into her portable cassette player.

HILLY

Wait. I'm still working on the lights and music.
All they offer on the intercom is a choice between classical and popular. This is the classical.

She presses a button by her bed and we HEAR the cannon
finale from Tchaikovsky's "1812."

HILLY

And this is the popular.

She presses another button and we hear Guy Lombardo playing "The Donkey Serenade."

GEORGE

That's the popular? I think we're in a time warp.

George has taken off his coat and tie and goes to the bathroom to get a towel for the champagne. Hilly puts her cassette player down by the bed and turns it on.

HILLY

So I'm settling for this.

From the cassette player we hear the lilting love song known
as "Hilly's Theme."

GEORGE

Beautiful.

He comes out of the bathroom and sits beside her on the bed.

GEORGE

I love that song. And now whenever I hear it
I'll be thinking of you.

He leans over and kisses her softly on the cheek. Hilly likes it.

HILLY

You put that very nicely.

GEORGE

Thank you. Some champagne?

HILLY

Please.

George begins undoing one of the bottles.

(21)

GEORGE

I can't get over the size of this place with the partition down.

HILLY

They are small rooms individually . . . but perfect for juggling.

GEORGE

For what?

HILLY

Juggling. When you practice the balls would always bounce off the walls.

She demonstrates with three imaginary balls. George smiles and pops the cork. He fills the glasses.

GEORGE

You juggle a lot?

HILLY
(slyly)

I know what goes where—and why.

George stops, looks her in the eye, and she smiles back innocently. He grins and they begin chuckling with an easy fun-filled sensuality. George offers her a glass of champagne.

> GEORGE
>
> Yours.

> HILLY
>
> Thank you.

> GEORGE
>
> And mine.

He leans back on the bed and they face each other.

> GEORGE
>
> To us. And the romance of the railroad.

> HILLY
>
> Trains that pass in the night.

They sip.

> HILLY
>
> Why don't you take your shoes off? You're sup-

(22)

> posed to put them in that little locker and the porter will have them shined for you in the morning.

> GEORGE
>
> Really? That's terrific.

While taking off his shoes he glances at the Rembrandt book on the chair.

> GEORGE
>
> This the master's work?

HILLY

Uh huh. He gave me that copy for safekeeping.
Want to read it?

George puts his shoes in the little locker near the door.

GEORGE

Later.

He turns off the overhead lights, leaving on the blue nıgnt
lights and the orange reading lamps. It is a romantic combination and Hilly smiles her approval.

HILLY

Grab your pillow and we can look at the desert
in the moonlight.

GEORGE

Great idea.

George takes the pillow from his bed, which lies parallel with
the window, over to Hilly's bed, which lies vertical with the
window.

GEORGE

Slide over.

They snuggle on the bed so that they are both lying on their
backs with George's arm around Hilly's shoulder. For a
moment they just stare out the window, watching the cactus
and the desert hills of the Mojave zip by under the stars.

HILLY

Beautiful, isn't it?

GEORGE

Very.

He puts down his glass and kisses her hair. She rolls over and faces him.

(23)

HILLY

George?

GEORGE

Yes.

HILLY

Do you really edit sex manuals?

GEORGE

I really do. But I have a confession to make.

HILLY

Oh?

GEORGE

I'm actually much better at books on gardening.

HILLY
(smiling)

Really?

GEORGE

Oh, yes. That's my special field.

HILLY

An authority?

GEORGE

Absolutely.

Hilly begins unbuttoning his shirt.

HILLY
Well then, is there anything you might want to
pass on?

GEORGE
You mean a few tips on gardening techniques?

HILLY
Yes. Some helpful hints for the beginner.

GEORGE
Well, when gardening one rule to remember is—
be nasty to nasturtiums.

Hilly kisses his naked chest and giggles.

HILLY
Is that so?

(24)

GEORGE
Oh, yes.

HILLY
They like it rough, huh?

GEORGE
The rougher the better.

She kisses his chin.

HILLY
Great. What else should I know?

GEORGE
There's the secret for treating azaleas.

> HILLY
Tell me. I'm all ears.

She snuggles into his neck and begins biting his ear.

> GEORGE
Treat them the same as begonias.

> HILLY
No kidding?

> GEORGE
It's gospel.

> HILLY
> *(wanting to get it straight)*
So you're saying: "What's good for azaleas is good for begonias."

> GEORGE
I couldn't have expressed it better myself.

Hilly leans up on one elbow.

> HILLY
George, this is fascinating.

> GEORGE
Didn't I tell you.

> HILLY
I'd like to delve deeper.

> GEORGE
Be my guest.

(25)

She goes back to kissing his chest and begins working her way down toward his navel.

HILLY
Well, then, what would happen if you treated an
azalea like a nasturtium?

George glances at the window—and freezes.

NEW ANGLE—SHOCK CUT

Out the window the dead body of a man suddenly slams into
FRAME. He dangles grotesquely, held up by his coat caught
on a protruding bolt. George gasps. The train WHISTLE
screams.

We see clearly the face of the dead man—an older gentleman
with a white moustache and goatee. He has been beaten and
shot in the head and the blood trickles down the side of his
face.

George jumps off the bed. The body sways for another second
then falls away. The WHISTLE stops and all is still once
more.

INT. GEORGE'S COMPARTMENT—ANOTHER
ANGLE

Hilly has seen nothing but she looks up at George, staring
transfixed at the empty window.

HILLY
George. What is it? I'm sorry I asked the question.

GEORGE
Did you see that? That man?

George flips on the light and rushes to the window, trying to
look back down the tracks.

HILLY

What man?

GEORGE

There was a man out the window. He'd been shot in the head.

HILLY

What?

GEORGE
(very excitedly)
Hilly, I'm not joking. A dead man fell off the

(26)

roof. His coat was caught. I saw it. What should I do? I've got to report it. Maybe they can stop the train.

HILLY

Hey, hey, hey! Lighten up!

She gets off the bed and takes hold of him.

HILLY

C'mon now. Sit down. You need a little more champagne.

GEORGE

I'm not kidding, Hilly. I saw it.

HILLY

Okay. Here.

George sits and Hilly pours him some champagne. George drinks it down in one gulp.

GEORGE
Wow! I can't believe it.

HILLY
Me neither.

GEORGE
But I saw it, really I did.

HILLY
Of course you did. You saw something. But who knows what it was. An old newspaper. A kid's kite. A Halloween mask. It could have been anything.

GEORGE
No, I'm sure it was a body—a dead man. His eyes were so clear.

HILLY
More clear than your head. George, you imagined it.

GEORGE
No, I'm positive I didn't.

HILLY
All right then, call the conductor and tell him your story. We've still got another bottle of champagne.

(27)

GEORGE
He'll think I've been drinking.

HILLY

Where would he get that idea?

GEORGE

But, Hilly, it was so vivid.

HILLY

Come here.

Hilly fluffs up his pillow and urges him to put his legs up. George rubs his forehead.

GEORGE

Wow, I feel kind of dizzy.

HILLY

Lie down.

George falls back on the bed with a sigh. Hilly picks up the cassette recorder, which stopped playing when George knocked it over, and looks around for a place where it will be safe. She starts the music ("Hilly's Theme") and puts it on a high overhanging rack near the window.

GEORGE

Boy, if that's what the DTs are like, I'm giving up the bottle for life.

HILLY

The mind plays funny tricks all the time. You know that. Just relax and forget it.

Hilly turns off the lights and lies alongside George. He looks at her for a long moment.

GEORGE

That sure is a pretty song.

HILLY

Yes, it is.

He kisses her gently on the lips and then looks at her with a great deal of tenderness.

GEORGE

You are very beautiful, Hilly.

Hilly despite her sophistication is not used to this tenderness. Tears well in her eyes.

(28)

HILLY

I like you, too.

He moves forward again and they kiss long and passionately. This is the first time they have showed their real need and mutual desire and when the kiss is broken they both look at each other knowing that this feeling between them is truly something special.

GEORGE

Are you sure I'm not dreaming?

HILLY

Maybe we both are.

She falls into his arms and he hugs her longingly.

Notice how the scene incorporates a beginning, middle, and end. This is also the plot point at the end of Act I, so find "the incident or event" that takes us into Act II. Notice the subtly expressed warmth between the two characters. On screen, Wilder and Clayburgh breathed life into it, and it became a lovely moment.

It's a perfect example of a scene that works!

*   *   *

As an exercise: Create a scene by creating a *context* and then establishing *content*. Find the *purpose* of the scene, then choose the *place* and *time* for the scene. Find the *components* or *elements* within the scene to create conflict and dimension and to generate drama. Drama, remember, is conflict; seek it out.

Your story always moves forward, step by step, scene by scene, toward the resolution.

11

Building the Screenplay

Wherein we discuss constructing the screenplay:

Up until now, we've discussed the four basic elements needed to write a screenplay—ending, beginning, plot point at the end of Act I, and plot point at the end of Act II. Those are the four things you need to know before you put one word on paper.

Now what?

How do you go about putting all those things together to build a screenplay?

How do you construct a screenplay?

Take a look at the *paradigm*:

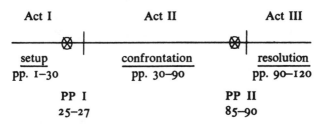

Act I, Act II, Act III. Beginning, middle, and end. Each act is a *unit*, or *block*, of dramatic action.

Look at Act I:

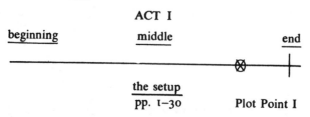

ACT I

beginning   middle   end

the setup
pp. 1–30   Plot Point I

Act I extends from the *opening* of the screenplay to the *plot point* at the end of Act I. Therefore, there is a beginning of the *beginning*, a middle of the *beginning*, and an end of the *beginning*. It is a self-contained *unit*, a block of dramatic action. It is approximately 30 pages long, and about page 25 or 27 a *plot point* occurs, an incident or event that "hooks" into the action and spins it around into another direction. What happens in Act I is the dramatic context known as the *setup*. You have approximately 30 pages to *set up* your story; introduce the *main character*, state the *dramatic premise*, and *establish the situation*, visually and dramatically.

Here's Act II:

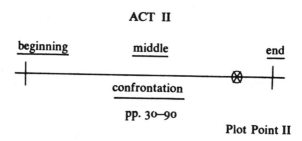

ACT II

beginning   middle   end

confrontation

pp. 30–90

Plot Point II

Act II is the *middle* of your screenplay. It contains the bulk of action. It goes from the beginning of Act II to the plot point at the end of Act II. So, we have a beginning of the *middle*, a middle of the *middle*, and an end of the *middle*.

It is also a *unit*, or block, of dramatic action. It is approximately 60 pages long, and about page 85–90 another plot point occurs which "spins" the story around into Act III. The dramatic *context* is confrontation, and your character will encounter obstacles that keep him from reaching his goal. (Once you determine the "need" of your character, create obstacles to that need. Conflict! Your story then becomes your character overcoming all obstacles to achieve his or her "need.")

Act III is the end, or resolution, of your screenplay.

ACT III

beginning	middle	end

resolution

pp. 90–120

Like Acts I and II, there is a beginning of the *end*, a middle of the *end*, and an end of the *end*. It is approximately 30 pages long, and the dramatic *context* is the *resolution* of your story.

In each act, you start from the beginning of the act and move toward the plot points at the end of the act. That means each act has a *direction*, a line of development from beginning to the plot point. The plot points at the end of Acts I and II are your destination points; that's where you're going when you're building or constructing a screenplay.

You build your screenplay in terms of units—Act I, II, III.

How do you build your screenplay?

Use 3 × 5 cards.

Take a pack of 3 × 5 cards. Write the idea for each scene or sequence on a single card, and maybe a few brief words of description to aid you when you're writing. For example, if you have a sequence about your character in a hospital, you can indicate several scenes, one per card: *arrival* of your character at the hospital; *he or she checks in* at the admitting office; the *doctors examine him*; lab work is done; various medical tests, like X rays, EKG, or EEG, are conducted; family members or friends visit him; his hospital roommate may be someone he dislikes; the doctors might discuss the case with relatives; your character might be in the intensive care unit. All this can be specified in a few words on each card. Each description can be written into a scene, all within the sequence marked "Hospital."

You can use as many cards as you like: Edward Anhalt, who adapted *The Young Lions* and *Becket,* uses 52 cards to build his screenplays. That's how many cards there are in a package. Ernest Lehman, who wrote *North by Northwest, The Sound of Music,* and *Family Plot,* uses anywhere from 50 to 100, however many he needs. Frank Pierson wrote *Dog Day Afternoon* in 12 cards; he wove the story around 12 basic sequences. Again, there is no rule about how many cards you need to have to build your screenplay; use as many as you want. You can also use different-colored cards: blue for Act I, green for Act II, and yellow for Act III.

Your story determines how many cards you need. Trust your story! Let *it* tell you how many cards you need, whether it be 12, 48, 52, 80, 96, 118; it doesn't matter. Trust your story.

The cards are an incredible method. You can arrange scenes any way you want, rearrange them, add some, omit others. It is a method that is simple, easy, and effective, and gives you maximum mobility in building your screenplay.

Let's begin to build a screenplay by creating the dramatic *context* of each act, so we can find the *content.*

Remember Newton's Third Law of Motion from physics —"for every action there is an equal and opposite reaction." The principle works in building the screenplay. First, you must know the *need* of your main character. What is the *need* of your character? What does he or she want to achieve, get, satisfy, or win, within the body of your screenplay? Once you establish your character's need, then you can create obstacles to that need.

Drama is conflict.

And the essence of character is action—action is character.

We live in a world of action-reaction. If you're driving a car (action) and someone cuts you off or cuts in front of you, what do you do (reaction)? Swear, usually. Honk your horn indignantly. Try to cut the other driver off, tailgate him. Shake your fist, mutter to yourself, step on the gas! It's all a *reaction* to the *action* of the driver cutting you off.

Action-reaction, it's a law of the universe. If your character *acts* in your screenplay, somebody, or something, is going to *react* in such a way that your character *reacts*. Then, he will usually create a *new* action that will create another reaction.

Your character *acts*, and somebody *reacts*. Action-reaction, reaction-action—your story always moves toward that plot point at the end of each act.

Many new or inexperienced writers have things happening to their characters, and they are always *reacting* to their situation, rather than *acting* in terms of dramatic need. The essence of character is *action*; your character must *act*, not react.

In *Three Days of the Condor*, Act I sets up the office routine of Robert Redford. When Redford returns from lunch, everyone is dead. That is the plot point at the end of

Act I. Redford *reacts*: he calls the CIA; they tell him to avoid all places where he's known, especially home. He finds the absent coworker dead in bed, and doesn't know where to go or whom to trust. He is *reacting* to the situation. He *acts* when he phones Cliff Robertson and tells him he wants his friend Sam to meet him and bring him into headquarters. When that fails, Redford *acts* by forcing Faye Dunaway to take him to her apartment at gunpoint: He's got to rest, collect his thoughts, find out what action to take.

Action is *doing* something, *reacting* is having it happen.

In *Alice Doesn't Live Here Anymore*, Alice, after the death of her husband, is going to Monterey, California, to become a singer and satisfy a childhood dream. In order to survive with her young son, she seeks a job as a singer in various bars. At first no one will give her a chance. She becomes desperate, despondent, hoping for a break. She is *reacting* to her situation—the circumstances surrounding her —and this makes her a passive and not very sympathetic character. When she does get a chance to sing, it's not what she expected at all.

Many inexperienced writers have things happen to their characters; they *react* rather than act. The essence of character is *action*.

You've got 30 pages to set up your story, and the first ten pages are crucial.

Within the first ten pages, you must establish the *main character*, set up the dramatic *premise*, and establish the *situation*.

You know what your opening is, and you know the plot point at the end of the first act. It's either a scene or a sequence, an "incident" or an "event."

If you think about it, you've already got about five or ten pages of your script written with those two elements. So, you've got about 20 pages to write in order to complete Act I. Not bad, especially since you haven't written anything yet. Now you're ready to build your screenplay. Start with Act I.

It is a complete unit of dramatic action; it begins with the opening scene or sequence and ends at the plot point at the end of the act.

Take the 3 × 5 cards. Write down a few words or descriptive phrases on each card. If it's an office sequence, write "office," and what happens there: "embezzlement of $250,000 discovered." On another card: "emergency meeting of top executives." The next card: "introduce Joe as main character." Next card: "the media learn about it."

Next card: "Joe nervous, insecure." Use as many cards as you need to make the "office sequence" complete.

What happens next?

Take another card and write the next scene: "Joe questioned by police."

Then what happens?

A scene with "Joe and family at home." Another card: "Joe receives phone call; he is a suspect."

Next card: "Joe driving to work." Next card: "Joe arrives at work, the strain evident."

What happens next?

"Joe questioned further by police." A scene can be added where the "media question Joe." Another card: "Joe's family knows he's innocent; will stick by him." Another card: "Joe with attorney. Things look bad."

Step by step, scene by scene, build your story to the plot point at the end of the act; "Joe indicted for embezzlement." That's the plot point at the end of Act I. It's like putting together a jigsaw puzzle.

You may have 8, 10, 14 or more cards for Act I. You've indicated the flow of dramatic action to the plot point. When you've completed the cards for Act I, take a look at what you've got. Go over the cards, scene by scene, like flash cards. Do it several times. Soon you pick up a definite flow of action; you'll change a few words here and a few words there to make it read easier. Get used to the story line. Tell yourself the story of the first act, the *setup*.

If you want to write a few extra cards because you discover a few holes in your story, do so. The cards are for you. Use them to construct your story, so you always know where you're going.

When you've completed the cards for Act I, put them on a bulletin board, on the wall or on the floor, in sequential order. Tell yourself the story from the beginning to the plot point at the end of Act I. Do it over and over again, and pretty soon you'll begin to weave the story into the fabric of the creative process.

Do the same with Act II. Use the plot point at the end of the act to guide you. List the sequences you have lined up for the act.

Remember the dramatic *context* of Act II is *confrontation*. Is your character moving through the story with his "need" firmly established? You must keep obstacles in mind all the time in order to generate dramatic conflict.

When you've finished the cards, repeat the process from Act I; go through the cards from the beginning of Act II to the plot point at the end of Act II. Free-associate, let ideas come to you, put them on cards and go over and over them.

Lay them out. Study them. Plot your story progression. See how it's working. Don't be afraid to change anything. A film editor I once interviewed told me an important creative principle; he said that within the context of the story "the sequences tried that *don't work* are the ones that tell you *what does work*."

It's a classic rule in film. Many of the best cinematic moments happen by accident. A scene *tried* that doesn't work when first tried will ultimately tell you what *does* work.

Don't be afraid to make mistakes.

How long should you spend on the cards?

About a week. It takes me four days to lay out the cards. I spend one full day on Act I, about four hours. I spend two days on Act II; the first day for the first half of the act, the second day for the last half. And, one day laying out Act III.

Then, I'll put them on the floor or bulletin board. I'm ready to start working.

I spend a few weeks going over and over the cards, getting to know the story, the progression, the characters, until I feel comfortable. That means about two to four hours a day spent with the cards. I'll go through the story, act by act, scene by scene, shuffling cards around, trying something here, moving one scene from Act I into Act II, a scene from Act II into Act I. The card method is so flexible you can do anything you want, and it works!

The card system allows you maximum mobility in structuring your screenplay. Go over and over the cards until you feel ready to begin writing. How do you know when to start writing? You'll know; it's a feeling you get. When you're ready to start writing, you'll start writing. You'll feel secure with your story; you'll know what you need to do, and you'll start getting visual images of certain scenes.

Is the card system the only way to construct your story?

No. There are several ways to do it. Some writers simply list a series of scenes on the page, numbering them (1) Bill at the office; (2) Bill with John at bar; (3) Bill sees Jane; (4) Bill leaves for party; (5) Bill meets Jane; (6) they like each other, decide to leave together.

Another way is to write a *treatment*; a *narrative synopsis* of what happens in your story incorporating a little dialogue; a treatment is anywhere from 4 to 20 pages long. An *outline* is also used, especially in television, where you tell your story in a detailed narrative plot progression; dialogue is an essential part of the *outline*, and it is anywhere from 28 to 60 pages in length. Most *outlines*, or *treatments*, should not be longer than 30 pages. Do you know why?

The producer's lips get tired.

That's an old Hollywood joke, and there's a great deal of truth to it.

No matter what method you use, you are now ready to move from telling the story on cards to writing the story on paper.

You know your story from start to finish. It should move smoothly from beginning to end, with plot progression clearly in mind so all you have to do is look at the cards, close your eyes, and *see* the story unfolding.

All you've got to do is write it!

*   *   *

As an exercise: Determine your ending, opening, and plot point at the end of Acts I and II. Get some 3 × 5 cards, different colors if you choose, and start with the opening of your screenplay. Free-associate. Whatever comes to mind for a scene, put it down on the cards. Build toward the plot point at the end of the act.

Experiment with it. The cards are for you—find your own method to make them work for your story. You might want to write a *treatment* or *outline*. Do it.

12

Writing the Screenplay

Wherein we talk about "doing it":

The hardest thing about writing is knowing what to write.

Look back and take a look where we've come from. Here's the *paradigm:*

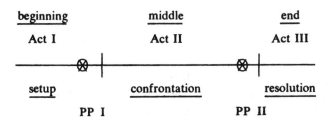

We've talked about a *subject,* like three guys holding up the Chase Manhattan Bank, and broken it down into *action* and *character.* We talked about choosing a *main* character, and two *major* characters, and channeling their action into robbing the bank. We talked about choosing our *ending,* our *beginning,* and the *plot points* at the end of Acts I and II. We've talked about *constructing the screenplay* with 3 × 5 cards, and are familiar with the *direction* of the story.

167 ✱

Look at the *paradigm*: WE KNOW WHAT TO WRITE!
We have completed a form of preparation applicable to all
writing in general, and the screenplay in particular; it is form
and structure. You are now able to select the elements of
your story that fall inside the *paradigm* of screenplay form.
In other words, you know *what* to write; all you've got to do
is *write it!*

Writing a screenplay is an amazing, almost mysterious
phenomenon. One day you're up on top of things, the next
day you're down, lost in confusion and uncertainty. One day
it works, the next day it doesn't; who knows how or why. It is
the creative process; it defies analysis; it is magic and it is
wonder.

Whatever has been said or written about the experience of
writing from the beginning of time, it still boils down to one
thing—writing is your own, personal experience. Nobody
else's.

A lot of people contribute to the making of a movie, but
the writer is the only person who sits down and faces the
blank sheet of paper.

Writing is hard work, a day-by-day job, sitting in front of
your pad or typewriter day in, day out, getting words down
on paper. You've got to put in the time.

Before you begin writing, you've got to *find the time* to
write.

How many hours a day do you need to spend writing?

That depends on you. I work about four hours a day, five
days a week. John Milius writes one hour a day, seven days a
week, between 5 and 6 P.M. Stirling Silliphant, who wrote
The Towering Inferno, sometimes writes 12 hours a day.
Paul Schrader works on a story in his head for months, telling it to people until he *knows* it completely; then he "jumps

in" and writes it in about two weeks. Then, he'll spend weeks polishing and fixing it.

You need two to three hours a day to write a screenplay. Look at your daily schedule. Examine your time. If you're working full time, or caring for home and family, your time is limited. You're going to have to find the best time for you to write. Are you the kind of person who works best in the morning? Or does it take you until early afternoon to be wide awake and alert? Late at night may be a good time. Find out.

You may get up and write a few hours before you go to work; or, come home from work, unwind, and then write a few hours. You may want to work at night, say about 10 or 11 P.M., or you may go to bed early and wake up about 4 A.M. to write. If you're a housewife and have a family, you may want to write when everyone's gone for the day, either midmorning, or midafternoon. You be the judge of what time, day or night, you can get two to three hours alone.

And a few hours alone is a few hours alone. No telephone, no friends for coffee, no idle chatter, no chores, no demands made on you by husbands, wives, lovers, or children. You need two to three hours alone, without interruption.

It may take you a while to find the "right" time. Fine. Experiment, make sure it's the best time for you to work.

Writing is a day-by-day job. You write your screenplay shot by shot, scene by scene, page by page, day by day. Set goals for yourself. Three pages a day is reasonable and realistic. That's almost 1,000 words a day. If a screenplay is 120 pages long, and you write three pages a day, five days a week, how long will it take you to write a first draft?

Forty working days. If you work five days a week, that means you can get a first draft in about six weeks. Once you start the writing process, you'll have days when you write ten pages, days when you do six, and so on. Just make sure you get three pages a day. Or more.

If you're married, or in a relationship, it's going to be difficult—you need some space and private time, as well as support and encouragement.

Housewives usually have a more difficult time than others. Husbands and children are not very understanding or supportive. No matter how many times you explain that you're "going to be writing," it doesn't help. Demands are made on you that are difficult to ignore. Many of my married women students tell me their husbands threaten to leave them unless they stop writing; their children turn into "animals." Husbands and children know their domestic routine is being interfered with, and they don't like it; often, unintentionally of course, they'll gang up on "Mother," who simply wants some time, space, and freedom. It's tough to handle; emotions of guilt, anger, or frustration get in the way and if you don't watch out you could easily become a victim of your emotions.

When you're in the writing experience, you're near your loved ones in body, but your mind and concentration are a thousand miles away. Your family doesn't care or understand that your characters are in a highly charged dramatic situation; *you* can't break your concentration to deal with the snacks, meals, laundry, and shopping that you normally do.

Don't expect to. If you're in a relationship your loved ones will *tell* you they understand and support you, but they won't —not really. Not because they don't want to, but because they don't understand the writing experience.

Don't feel "guilty" about taking the time *you need* to write your screenplay. If you expect your wife, husband, or lover to "get upset," or "not understand" when you're writing, it won't bother you when it happens. *If* it does. You have to be "at choice" when you're writing; expect a "tough time" and it won't bother you if it happens.

A note to all husbands, wives, lovers, friends, and children: If your husband, wife, lover, or parent is writing a screenplay, they need your love and support.

Give them the opportunity to explore their desire to write a screenplay. During the time they're writing, anywhere from three to six months, they're going to be moody, explosive, easily upset, preoccupied, and distant. Your daily routine is going to be interfered with, and you're not going to like it. It's going to be uncomfortable.

Are you willing to give them the space and the opportunity to write what they want to write? Do you love them enough to support them in their efforts even if it interferes with your life?

If the answer is "no," talk about it. Work out a way so that both sides can win, and then support each other. Writing is a lonely, solitary job. For a person in a relationship, it becomes a joint experience.

Establish a writing schedule: 10:30 to 12 noon; or 8 to 10 P.M.; or 9 to midnight. With a schedule, the "problem" of discipline becomes easier to handle.

Decide *how many* days you're going to be writing. If you're working full time, at school, or involved in a marriage or relationship, you can't expect to write a screenplay working one or two days a week. Creative energy is lost that way. You've got to focus and concentrate clearly on the script you're writing. You need at least four days a week.

With your writing schedule set up you can get down to work; and one fine day you sit down to write.

What's the first thing that's going to happen?

Resistance, that's what.

After you write FADE IN: EXT. STREET—DAY, you'll suddenly be seized with an incredible "urge" to sharpen your pencils or clean your work area. You'll find a *reason* or *excuse* not to write. That's resistance.

Writing is an experiential process, a learning process involving the acquisition of skill and coordination; like riding a bicycle, swimming, dancing, or playing tennis.

Nobody learns to swim by being thrown into the water. You learn to stay afloat, to survive. You learn to swim by perfecting your form, and you can only do that by actually swimming; the more you do the better you get.

It's the same thing with writing. You're going to experience some form of resistance. It shows itself in many ways and most of the time we aren't even aware it's happening.

For example: When you first sit down to start writing you may want to clean the refrigerator. Or wash the kitchen floor. You may want to jog, change the sheets, take a drive, eat, or have sex. Some people go out and buy $500 worth of clothes they don't want! Or, get angry, impatient, and yell at everybody and anybody for nothing in particular.

They're all forms of resistance.

One of my favorite forms of resistance is sitting down to write and suddenly getting an idea for *another* screenplay. A *much better* idea; an idea so original, so exciting, you wonder what you're doing writing "this" screenplay. You really think about it.

You may get two or three "better" ideas. It happens quite often; it may be a great idea, but it's a form of resistance! If it's really a good idea, it will keep. Simply write it up in a page or two and file it away. If you decide to pursue this "new" idea and abandon the original project, you'll discover the same thing happening; when you sit down to write, you'll get *another new idea,* and so on and so on. It's resistance; a mind-trip, a way of avoiding writing.

We all do it. We're masters at creating *reasons* and *excuses* not to write; it's simply a "barrier" to the creative process. How do you deal with it? Simple. If you know it's going to happen, simply acknowledge it when it does. When you're cleaning the refrigerator, sharpening pencils, or eating, just know that's what you're doing; experiencing resistance! It's no big thing. Don't put yourself down, feel guilty, or punish yourself. Just acknowledge the resistance—then you move right through to the other side. Just don't *pretend* it's *not happening*. It is! Once you deal with your resistance, you're ready to start writing.

The first ten pages are the most difficult. Your writing is going to be awkward and probably not very good. It's okay. Some people won't be able to deal with that; they'll make a decision that what they're writing is no good. They'll stop, righteous and justified, because they "knew they couldn't do it."

Writing is a learning coordination; the more you do the easier it gets.

At first, your dialogue's probably not going to be very good.

Remember that dialogue is a function of character. Let's review the purpose of dialogue. It
—moves the story forward;
—communicates facts and information to the reader;
—reveals character;
—establishes character relationships;
—makes your characters real, natural, and spontaneous;
—reveals the conflicts of the story and characters;
—reveals the emotional states of your characters; and
—comments on the action.

Your first attempts will probably be stilted, clichéd, fragmented, and strained. Writing dialogue is like learning to swim; you're going to flounder around, but the more you do the easier it gets.

It takes anywhere from 25 to 50 pages before your characters start talking to you. And they *do* start talking to you. Don't worry about the dialogue. Just keep writing. Dialogue can always be cleaned up.

Those of you looking for "inspiration" to guide you won't find it. Inspiration is measured in moments, a few minutes, or hours, a screenplay in weeks and months. If it takes you 100 days to write a screenplay, and you're "on" for 10 of those days, consider yourself lucky. Being "on" for 100 days, or 25 days, just doesn't happen. You may "hear" that it does, but in truth it's the pot at the end of the rainbow—you're chasing a dream.

"But"—you say.

But what?

Writing is a day-by-day job, two to three hours a day, three or four days a week, three pages a day, ten pages a week. Shot by shot, scene by scene, page by page, sequence by sequence, act by act.

When you're *in* the *paradigm*, you can't *see* the *paradigm*.

The card system is your map and your guide, the plot points your checkpoints along the way, the "last-chance" gas station before you hit the high desert, the ending, your destination. What's nice about the card system is that you can forget it. The cards have served their purpose. At the typewriter, or pad, you'll suddenly "discover" a new scene that works better, or hadn't been thought of. Use it.

It doesn't matter if you want to drop scenes or add new ones; do it. Your creative mind has assimilated the cards so you can throw out a few scenes and still be following the *direction* of your story.

When you're doing the cards, you're doing the cards. When you're writing, you're writing. Forget a rigid adherence to the cards. Let them guide you, don't be a slave to them. If, at the typewriter, you feel a spontaneous moment that gives you a better, more fluid story, write it.

Keep writing. Day by day, page by page. And during the writing process you're going to discover things about yourself you never knew. For example, if you're writing about something that happened to you, you may re-experience some of those old feelings and emotions. You may get "wacky" and irritable and live each day as if you were on an emotional roller coaster. Don't worry. Just keep writing.

You're going to move through three stages of your first-draft screenplay.

The first stage is the "words on paper" stage. This is when you put it all down. If you're in doubt about writing a scene or not writing it, write it. If in doubt, write. That's the rule. If you start censoring yourself you might wind up with a 90-page screenplay, and that's too short. You'll have to add scenes to a tight structure to bring it to length, and that's difficult. It's easier to cut scenes out than add them to an already structured screenplay.

Keep moving forward in your story. If you write a scene and go back to clean it up, to polish it and "make it right," you'll find you've dried up about page 60, and might shelve the project. Many writers I know who've tried to write a draft this way have failed to complete it. Any major changes you need to make, do in the second draft.

There will be moments when you don't know how to begin a scene, or what to do next. You know the scene on cards, but not how to get into it visually.

Ask yourself "what happens, next?" and you'll get an answer. It's usually the *first* thought skittering across your mind. Grab it, and throw it down on paper. It's what I call the "creative grab," because you've got to be quick enough to "catch it" and put it down.

Many times you'll try to improve that first idea to "make it better." If your first thought is to have the scene in a car driving down the highway, and you decide to make it a walk in the country or a walk on the beach, you'll lose a certain creative energy. Do it too many times and your script will reflect a "contrived," deliberate quality. It won't work.

There's only one rule that governs your writing; not whether it's "good" or "bad," but does it work? Does your scene work? If it does, keep it in, no matter what anybody says.

If it works, use it. If it doesn't, don't.

If you don't know how to get in or out of a scene, free-associate. Let your mind wander; ask yourself the best way to get into the scene; trust yourself; you'll find the answer.

If you created a problem, you'll be able to find a solution to that problem. All you have to do is look for it.

Problems in a screenplay can always be solved. If you created it, you can solve it. If you're stuck, go back to your people; go into your character biography and ask your character what he or she would do in that situation. You'll get an answer. It may take a minute, an hour, a day, several days, a week, but you'll get the answer; probably when you least expect it, and in the most unusual place. Just keep asking yourself the question: "What do I need to do to solve this problem?" Run it through your head constantly, especially before you go to sleep. Occupy yourself with it. You'll find an answer.

Writing is the ability to ask yourself questions and get the answers.

Sometimes you'll get into a scene and not know where you're going, or what you're looking for to make it work. You know the *context*, not the *content*. So you'll write the same scene five different times, from five different points of view, and out of all these attempts you may find one line that gives you the key to what you're looking for.

You'll rewrite the scene using that one line as your anchor thought, and eventually be able to create something dynamic and spontaneous. You just have to find your way.

And trust yourself.

Around page 80 or 90, the resolution is forming and you'll discover the screenplay is literally writing itself. You're just like a medium, putting in time to finish the script. You don't have to do anything; it writes itself.

Does this method work in adapting a book, or novel, into a screenplay?

Yes.

When you adapt a book or novel into a screenplay, you must consider it an *original* screenplay *based* on other material. You can't adapt a novel literally and have it work, as Francis Ford Coppola learned when he adapted *The Great Gatsby* by F. Scott Fitzgerald. Coppola—*Patton, The Godfather, Apocalypse Now*—is one of the most arresting and dynamic writer-directors in Hollywood. In adapting *The Great Gatsby* he wrote a screenplay that is absolutely faithful to the novel. The result is a visually magnificent failure. Dramatically, it didn't work at all.

It's an apples-and-oranges situation.

When you adapt a book into a screenplay, all you need to use are the main characters, the situation, and some, but not all, of the story. You may have to add new characters, drop others, create new incidents or events, perhaps alter the entire structure of the book. In *Julia* Alvin Sargent created an entire movie out of an episode from *Pentimento* by Lillian Hellman.

Writing a screenplay is writing a screenplay. There are no shortcuts.

It may take you six to eight weeks to complete your first "words on paper" draft. Then you're ready to move into the second stage of your first draft; taking a cold, hard, objective look at what you've written.

This is the most mechanical and uninspiring stage of writing a screenplay. You'll take what is perhaps a 180–200 page draft of your script and reduce it to 130–140 pages. You'll cut out scenes, add new ones, rewrite others, and make any changes you need to get it into a workable form. It might take you about three weeks to do this. When you're finished, you're ready to approach the third stage of your first-draft script. This is where you see what you've got, where the story really gets written. You'll polish it, accent it, hone and rewrite it, trim to length, and make it all come to life. You're out of the *paradigm* now so you can see what you've got to do to make it better. In this stage you may rewrite a scene as many as ten times before you get it right.

There will always be one or two scenes that don't work the way you want them to, no matter how many times you rewrite them. You know these scenes don't work, but the reader will never know. He reads for story and execution, not content. I used to read a script in 40 minutes, seeing it in my head, rather than reading it for prose style or content. Don't worry about the few scenes you know don't work. Let them be.

You discover the scenes you like the *most*, those clever, witty, and sparkling moments of action and dialogue, might have to be cut when you reduce it to workable length. You'll *try* to keep them in—after all, it *is* your *best* writing—but in the long run you've got to do what's best for your screenplay. I have a "best scene" file where I put the "best" things I've ever written. I had to cut them out to tighten the script.

You have to learn to be ruthless writing a screenplay, to sometimes cut out what you know is the best thing you've ever written; if it doesn't work, it doesn't work. If your scenes stand out and draw attention to themselves, they might impede the flow of action. Scenes that stand out *and* work are the scenes that will be remembered. Every good film has one or, possibly, two scenes people always remember. These scenes work within the dramatic context of the story. They are also the trademark scenes that later become immediately recognizable. In *High Anxiety* Mel Brooks made a movie out of famous Alfred Hitchcock scenes. As a reader, I could always spot variations on "famous scenes" from the movie past. They usually don't work.

If you don't know whether your "choice" scenes work, they probably don't. If you have to think about it, or question it, it means it's not working. You'll know when a scene's working. Trust yourself.

Keep writing; day by day, page by page. The more you do the easier it gets. When you're almost finished, perhaps 10 or 15 pages from the end, you might find you're "holding on." You'll spend four days writing one scene or one page, and you'll feel tired and listless. It's a natural phenomenon; you simply don't want to finish it, to complete it.

Let it go. Just be aware you're "holding on," then let it go. One day you'll write "fade out, the end"—and you're done. *It's* done.

It's a time of celebration and relief. When it's over, you're going to experience all kinds of emotional reactions. First, satisfaction and relief. A few days later, you'll be down, depressed, and won't know what to do with your time. You may sleep a lot. You've got no energy. This is what I call the "postpartum blues" period. It's like giving birth to a baby; you've been working on something for a substantial period of time. It's been a part of you. It's gotten you up in the morning and kept you awake at night. Now it's over. It's natural to be down and depressed. The end of one thing is always the beginning of something else. Endings and beginnings, right?

It's all part of the experience of writing the screenplay.

13

Screenplay Form

*Wherein we illustrate the simplicity
of screenplay form:*

When I was head of the story department at Cinemobile, and reading an average of three screenplays a day, I could tell in the first paragraph whether the script was written by a professional or amateur. An abundance of CAMERA angles like long shots, close shots, instructions about zooms, pans, and dollies immediately revealed a novice screenwriter who didn't know what he or she was doing.

As a reader, I was always looking for an excuse not to read a script. So when I found one—like excessive CAMERA instructions—I used it. I didn't have to read ten pages. You can't sell a script in Hollywood without the help of a reader.

Don't give the reader an excuse not to read your screenplay.

That's what screenplay form is all about—what *is* a professional screenplay, and what *isn't*.

Everybody, it seems, has some misconceptions about screenplay form. Some people say if you're writing a screenplay you're "obligated" to write in CAMERA ANGLES; if you ask why they mumble something about "the director knowing *what* to film"! So they create an elaborate and meaningless exercise called "writing in CAMERA ANGLES."

It doesn't work.

Screenplay form is simple; so simple, in fact, that most people try to make it more complex. Richard Feynman, the Nobel Prize-winning physicist from Cal Tech, once remarked that "the laws of Nature are so simple, we have to rise above the complexity of scientific thought to see them." For every action there is an equal and opposite reaction. What could be more simple than that!

F. Scott Fitzgerald is a perfect example. Perhaps the most gifted American novelist of the twentieth century, Fitzgerald came to Hollywood to write screenplays. He failed miserably —he tried to "learn" CAMERA ANGLES and the intricate technology of film, and he let that get in the way of his screenwriting. Not one script he worked on was made without extensive rewriting. His only screenwriting achievement is unfinished, a script called *Infidelity* written for Joan Crawford in the 1930s. It's a beautiful script, patterned like a visual fugue, but the third act is incomplete and it lies gathering dust in the studio vaults.

Most people who want to write screenplays have a little of Scott Fitzgerald in them.

The screenwriter is *not responsible* for writing in CAMERA ANGLES, and detailed shot terminology. It's not the writer's job. The writer's job is to tell the director *what* to shoot, not *how* to shoot it. If you specify how each scene should be shot, the director will probably throw it away. Justifiably so.

The writer's job is to write the script. The director's job is to film the script; to take words on paper and transform them into images on film. The cameraman's function is to light the scene and position the camera so it cinematically captures the story.

I happened to be on the set of *Coming Home,* with Jane Fonda, Jon Voight, and Bruce Dern. Hal Ashby, the director, was rehearsing Jane Fonda and Penelope Milford in a scene, while Haskell Wexler, the director of photography, was preparing to set up the CAMERA.

Here's how it worked. Hal Ashby sat down in a corner with Jane Fonda and Penelope Milford and went over the context of the scene. Haskell Wexler was telling the crew where to put the lights. Ashby, Fonda, and Milford began blocking out the scene; she moves on this line, Penny enters on this cue, crosses to the bed, turns on the TV, and so on. Once the blocking was established, Haskell Wexler followed them with his "eyepiece," establishing the first camera angle. When Hal Ashby finished working with Fonda and Milford, Haskell Wexler showed him where he wanted to position the camera. Ashby agreed. They set up the camera, the actresses walked through the scene, rehearsed it several times, made minor adjustments, and were ready for a take.

That's the way it is. Film is a collaborative medium; people work together to create a movie. Don't worry about CAMERA ANGLES! Forget about writing scenes describing the intricate moves of a Panavision 70 camera with a 50mm lens on a Chapman crane!

There was a time, though, in the 1920s and '30s, when the director's job was to direct the actors, and it was the writer's job to write in CAMERA ANGLES for the cameraman. It's no longer true. It's not your job.

Your job is to write the script. Scene by scene, shot by shot.

What is a shot?

A shot is what the CAMERA sees.

Scenes are made up of shots, either a single shot or a series of shots; how many, or what kind, is insignificant. There are all kinds of shots. You can write a descriptive scene like "the sun rising over the mountains" and the director may use one, three, five, or ten different *shots* to visually get the feeling of the "sun rising over the mountains."

A scene is written in *master shot*, or *specific shots*. A master shot covers a *general area*; a room, a street, a lobby. A *specific shot* focuses on a specific part of the room, at the door, say, or in front of a specific store on a specific street, or building. The scenes from *Silver Streak* and *Chinatown* are presented in master shot. *Network* utilizes specific shots and master shots. If you want to write a dialogue scene in master shot, all you need to write is INT. RESTAURANT—NIGHT, and simply let your characters talk without any reference to the CAMERA or shot.

You can be as general, or specific, as you want. A scene can be one shot—a car racing down the street—or a series of shots of a couple arguing on the corner.

A shot is *what* the CAMERA sees.

Let's take another look at the screenplay form.

(1) EXT. ARIZONA DESERT—DAY

(2) A blazing sun scorches the earth. Everything is flat, barren. In the distance, a cloud of dust rises as a jeep makes its way across the landscape.

(3) MOVING

The jeep races through sagebrush and cactus.

(4) INT. JEEP—FAVORING JOE CHACO

(5)

Joe drives recklessly. JILL sits next to him, an attractive girl in her twenties.

(6) JILL
(7) (shouting)
(8) How far is it?

JOE
'Bout two hours. You okay?

(9) She smiles wearily.

JILL
I'll make it.

(10)

Suddenly, the motor SPUTTERS. They look at each other, concerned.

(11) CUT TO:

Simple, right!

This is the proper, contemporary, and professional screenplay form. There are very few rules, and these are the guidelines:

Line 1—called THE SLUG LINE is the general or specific locale. We are outside, EXT., somewhere in the ARIZONA DESERT; the time is DAY.

Line 2—double-space and then give your description of people, places, or action, single-spaced, from margin to margin. Descriptions of characters or places should not be longer than a few lines.

Line 3—double-space; the general term "moving" specifies a change in camera focus. (It is *not* a camera instruction. It is a "suggestion.")

Line 4—double-space; there is a change from *outside* the jeep, to *inside*. We are focusing on the character, Joe Chaco.

Line 5—New characters are always capitalized.

Line 6—The character speaking is always capitalized and placed in the center of the page.

Line 7—Stage directions for the actor are written in parentheses under the name of the character speaking. Always single-spaced. Don't abuse this; use only when necessary.

Line 8—Dialogue is placed in the center of the page, so the character speaking forms a block in the middle of the page surrounded by description from margin to margin. Several lines of dialogue are always single-spaced.

Line 9—Stage directions also include what characters do within the scene. Reactions, silent and otherwise.

Line 10—Sound effects, or music effects, are always capitalized. Don't overdo effects. The last step in the filmmaking process is to give the film to the music and effects editors. The film is "locked," that is, the picture track cannot be changed or altered. The editors skim through the script looking for music and effects cues, and you can help them by putting references to music or sound effects in capitals.

Film deals with two systems—the *film*, what we see, and the *sound*, what we hear. The film portion is complete before it goes to sound, and then the two are put together in sync. It is a long and complicated process.

Line 11—If you choose to indicate the end of a scene you may write "CUT TO:" or "DISSOLVE TO:" (*dissolve* means two images overlapping each other; one fades out as the other fades in) or "FADE OUT," used to indicate a fade to black. It should be noted that optical effects like "fades" or "dissolves" are really a film decision, made by the director or film editor. It is not the writer's decision.

That's all there is to basic screenplay form. It's simple.

It's a new form for most people who want to write screenplays, so give yourself time to "learn" how to write it. Don't be afraid to make mistakes. It takes a while to get used to it, and the more you do, the easier it gets. Sometimes I have students simply write, or type, ten pages of a screenplay just to get the "feel" of the form.

I once had a student who was a TV reporter for CBS News. He wanted to write a screenplay, but refused to learn the form. He wrote his script like a news story, even using the same paper. When I brought that to his attention, he said he'd change it after he finished the first draft. That was the way he wrote, he explained, and did not feel comfortable writing in any other style. And he wasn't going to change it. As it happened, he never finished his screenplay.

If you're going to write a screenplay, do it right! Write in screenplay form from the beginning. It's to your advantage.

The word CAMERA is rarely used in the contemporary screenplay. If your script is 120 pages long, there should be no more than a few references to CAMERA. Maybe ten. "But," people say, "if you don't use the word CAMERA and the shot is what the CAMERA sees, how do you write the shot description?"

The rule is: FIND THE SUBJECT OF YOUR SHOT!

What does the CAMERA, or the eye in the middle of your forehead, see? What takes place within the frame of each shot?

If Bill walks out of his apartment to his car, what is the subject of the shot?

Bill? The apartment? The car?

Bill is the subject of the shot.

If Bill gets in his car and drives down the street, what is the subject of the shot? Bill, the car, or the street?

The car is, unless you want the scene to take place inside the car: INT. CAR—DAY. Moving or not moving.

Once you determine the subject of the shot, you're ready to describe the visual action that takes place within the shot.

I've compiled a list of terms to replace the word CAMERA in your screenplay. If you're ever in doubt about whether to use the word CAMERA, *do not use it.* Find another term to replace it. These general terms used in shot descriptions will allow you to write your screenplay simply, effectively, and visually.

SCREENPLAY TERMS
(to replace the word CAMERA)

RULE: FIND THE SUBJECT OF YOUR SHOT.

TERM	MEANING
1. ANGLE ON (the subject of the shot)	A person, place, or thing— ANGLE ON BILL leaving his apartment building.
2. FAVORING (subject of the shot)	Also a person, place, or thing —FAVORING BILL as he leaves his apartment.
3. ANOTHER ANGLE	A variation of a SHOT—ANOTHER ANGLE of Bill walking out of his apartment.
4. WIDER ANGLE	A change of *focus* in a scene— You go from an ANGLE ON Bill to a WIDER ANGLE which now includes Bill and his surroundings.

5. NEW ANGLE

Another variation on a shot, often used to "break up the page" for a more "cinematic look"—A NEW ANGLE of Bill and Jane dancing at a party.

6. POV

A person's POINT OF VIEW, how something looks to him —ANGLE ON Bill, dancing with Jane, and from JANE'S POV Bill is smiling, having a good time. This could also be considered the CAMERA'S POV.

7. REVERSE ANGLE

A change in perspective, usually the opposite of the POV shot—For example, Bill's POV as he looks at Jane, and a REVERSE ANGLE of Jane looking at Bill—that is, what *she* sees.

8. OVER THE SHOULDER SHOT

Often used for POV and REVERSE ANGLE shots. Usually the back of a character's head is in the foreground of the *frame* and *what* he is looking at is the background of the frame. The *frame* is the boundary line of what the CAMERA sees—sometimes referred to as the "frame line."

9. MOVING SHOT

Focuses on the movement of a shot—A MOVING SHOT of the jeep racing across the

	desert. Bill walking Jane to the door. Ted *moves* to answer the phone. All you have to indicate is MOVING SHOT. Forget about trucking shots, pans, tilts, dollies, zooms, cranes.
10. CLOSE SHOT	What it says—close. Used sparingly, for emphasis. A CLOSE SHOT of Bill as he stares at Jane's roommate. When Jake Gittes, in *Chinatown*, has a knife in his nose, Robert Towne indicates a CLOSE SHOT. It is one of the few times he uses the term throughout the entire screenplay.
11. INSERT (of something)	A close shot of "something"— either a photograph, newspaper story, headline, face of a clock, watch, or telephone number is "inserted" into the scene.

Knowing these terms will help you write a screenplay from the position of choice and security—so you know what you're doing without the need of specific CAMERA directions.

Take a look at contemporary screenplay form. Here are the first nine pages of my screenplay *The Run*, an action film as yet unproduced. The opening is an action sequence. It is the story of a man setting out to break the Water Speed Record in a rocket boat.

Examine the form; look for the subject in each shot, and how each shot presents an individual mosaic within the tapestry of the sequence.

The "first time around" refers to the title of the individual sequence; it is the first attempt at breaking the Water Speed Record.

(page 1 of screenplay)

"THE RUN"

FADE IN:

"first time around"

EXT. BANKS LAKE, WASHINGTON—JUST BEFORE DAWN

A SERIES OF ANGLES

A few hours before dawn. Some stars and a full moon are pinned to the early-morning sky.

BANKS LAKE is a long sleeve of water nestled against the concrete walls of the Grand Coulee Dam. The water reflects the shimmering reflection of the moon. All is quiet. Peaceful. Hold.

Then, we HEAR the high-pitched ROAR of a truck. And, we:

CUT TO:

HEADLIGHTS—MOVING

A pickup truck moves INTO FRAME. PULL BACK to reveal the truck hauling a large trailer, the puzzling-shaped cargo covered with a tarpaulin. It could be anything—a piece of modern sculpture, a missile, a space capsule. As a matter of fact, it's all three.

A CARAVAN

of seven vehicles moves slowly along the winding, tree-lined highway. A pickup truck and station wagon lead the group. Another station wagon is followed by a truck and trailer. Bringing up the rear are two large camper trailers and a toolvan. They bear the insignia "Saga Men's Cologne."

INT. LEAD STATION WAGON

Three people are in the wagon. The radio plays softly, a Country & Western tune.

STRUT BOWMAN drives, a lean and expressive Texan who happens to be the best sheet-metal man and mechanical wizard west of the Mississippi.

JACK RYAN sits next to the window staring moodily into the predawn darkness.

(2)

Strong-willed and stubborn, he is considered by many to be a flamboyant boat designer, a crackpot genius, or a daredevil race driver; all three are true.

ROGER DALTON sits in the back seat. A quiet man, he wears glasses and looks like the rocket systems analyst he is.

THE VEHICLES

wind their way along the wood-lined highway heading toward the Grand Coulee Dam and the sleeve of water known as Banks Lake. (Formerly, it was known as Franklin D. Roosevelt Lake.)

EXT. BANKS LAKE—DAWN

The sky lightens as the caravan moves to the far side, the vehicles looking like a column of fireflies parading before the dawn.

THE BOATHOUSE AREA

The cars pull in and park. The lead truck pulls to a stop and a few CREW MEMBERS jump out. Others follow and the activity begins.

A long Quonset hut has been erected near the water. The BOATHOUSE, as it's known, houses the work area and is complete with work benches, lights, and tool area. The two campers park nearby.

A FEW CREWMEN

jump out and begin unloading various equipment, taking it into the work area.

THE STATION WAGON

Strut parks the wagon; Ryan is the first out, followed by Roger. He walks into the boathouse.

A TV CONTROL VAN

from "Sports World," as well as some local Seattle sports-casters, begin setting up their equipment.

THE OFFICIALS AND TIMERS

all with the initials FIA emblazoned on their shirts, set up electronic timing devices, timing boards, digital consoles, and floating timing buoys. Video images from the TV Control

Monitor are assembled into a montage of activity. The "feel" of this sequence should begin slowly, like someone waking up, then gradually build into a rhythm of a tense and exciting rocket-launch sequence.

(3)

INT. CAMPER LIVING QUARTERS—JUST AFTER DAWN

Jack Ryan puts on his asbestos racing suit and Strut helps him lace it up. He steps into his cover suit, the name of "Saga Men's Cologne" clearly seen. Strut fixes something on the suit, and the two men exchange a glance.

Over this, we HEAR the voice of the:

TV ANNOUNCER (VO)
This is Jack Ryan. Most of you already know the story—Ryan, one of the most innovative racing designers of high-speed water vehicles, son of the wealthy industrialist Timothy Ryan, was approached by Saga Men's Colognes to build a racing boat that would break the Water Speed Record of 286 miles an hour held by Leigh Taylor. Ryan did that and more: He designed and built the world's first rocket boat— that's right, rocket boat—revolutionary in concept and design—

THE BOATHOUSE

Moving out of the boathouse, mounted on two specially constructed mounts, is the rocket boat, "Prototype I," a gleaming, missile-like boat that looks like a Delta-winged aircraft. It is beautifully designed, a piece of sculpture. The crew members guide the boat onto the launching track, disappearing into the water. Over this, the TV announcer continues.

> TV ANNOUNCER (VO, contd.)
> Just how fast it will go is unknown—some people claim it won't even work! But Jack Ryan says this boat can easily break the 400 mi/hr barrier. Well, Ryan designed and built this boat, Prototype I, and took it to the sponsor. And, irony of ironies—Saga couldn't get anyone to drive the rocket boat—no one was willing to attempt the record in it—it was too radical, unsafe. That's when Ryan, the former hydroplane racer, stepped in and said, "I'll do it!"

INT. TV CONTROL VAN BOOTH

We see a bank of TV monitor screens. MOVE IN to a screen where the TV ANNOUNCER is interviewing Jack Ryan at a press conference.

(4)

> RYAN (on TV screen)
> You see, I built this boat, piece by piece—I know it like the back of my hand. If I thought there was the slightest chance of failure, or that I might possibly hurt myself, or kill myself—if I didn't think it was completely safe, I wouldn't do it! Somebody's got to do it and it might as well be me! I mean, that's what this life's all about, isn't it? Taking risks?

> TV ANNOUNCER (on screen)
> Are you scared?

> RYAN (on screen)
> Of course—but I know I can do the job. If I
> didn't, I wouldn't be here. It's my choice and I'm
> confident I'm going to set a new Water Speed
> Record and live long enough to give you a
> chance to interview me *after* I do it!

He laughs.

OLIVIA

Ryan's wife, standing nervously alone on the sidelines, biting
her lip. She's scared and she shows it.

EXT. TV CONTROL VAN—EARLY MORNING

The TV ANNOUNCER from the Ryan interview stands near
the Control Van, the lake in b.g.

> TV ANNOUNCER
> Several years ago, Jack Ryan was a highly suc-
> cessful hydroplane racer. He gave it up after an
> accident put him in the hospital—some of you
> remember that—

THE START AREA

A finger-like dock stretches into the water. A tow-boat is
tached to it.

(5)

PROTOTYPE I

sits on top of the water being fueled; two oxygen tanks connected with long polyethylene tubing disappear into the engine. Roger supervises the fueling.

RYAN

Jack Ryan steps out of the camper and walks toward the rocket boat. Strut is with him.

> TV ANNOUNCER (VO)
> So, here we are—at Banks Lake in eastern Washington, right next to the Grand Coulee Dam—where Jack Ryan becomes the first man in history to attempt setting a new Water Speed Record in a rocket boat.

AT THE START SITE

Ryan walks down the dock and steps into the boat.

AT TIMING CONTROL

A series of digital timing mechanisms race wildly, end at zero across the board.

INT. TV CONTROL BOARD IN VAN

The DIRECTOR sits in front of the TV Monitor Console and prepares for the TV broadcast. Eight screens are banked in front of him, each with a different image: crew, finish line, lake, timing buoys, crowd, etc. One screen follows Ryan as he prepares for the run.

> TV ANNOUNCER (VO)
> Working with Ryan are his two coworkers—
> Strut Bowman, the mechanical engineer—

STRUT

in the tow-boat, walkie-talkie in hand, watching Ryan carefully.

> TV ANNOUNCER (VO)
>> —and Roger Dalton, a rocket systems analyst,
>> and one of the scientists from the Jet Propulsion
>> Lab responsible for putting a man on the
>> moon—

ROGER

checking fuel gauges and other details. Everything's ready.

(6)

RYAN

is buckled into the cockpit. Strut is in the tow-boat, nearby.

INT. ROCKET BOAT COCKPIT

Ryan checks the three gauges on the control panel in front of
him. He flicks a toggle switch marked "fuel flow"; a needle
jumps into position and holds. He clicks another toggle
switch marked "water flow," and another needle is activated.
A red button switch lights up and we see the word "armed."
Ryan puts his hands on the steering wheel, positions one
finger next to the "eject" button.

RYAN

He checks the gauges, takes a few deep breaths. He's ready.

> TV ANNOUNCER (VO)
>> Ryan appears ready—

A SERIES OF ANGLES

of the countdown. Crews, timers, and spectators quiet down; electronic devices hold at zero; the TV camera crew is focused on Prototype I, poised like a bird on the edge of flight.

STRUT

watches Ryan, waits for him to give the "thumbs-up" signal.

RYAN

All we see are eyes peering out of a crash helmet. Concentration high, intention high.

THE TIMING COMPLEX

The timers wait, all eyes riveted on the timing mechanisms and the boat on the lake.

THE LAKE

is quiet, the metric-mile course marked out with three timing buoys.

AT THE FINISH LINE

Roger and two crewmen stand looking down course, watching the dot that is the boat.

THE TV CREW

waits, the air heavy with tense anticipation.

RYAN'S POV

He stares down course, the "armed" button clearly seen in foreground.

STRUT

checks and double-checks final details. Ryan's ready. He checks the timers—they're ready. It's a "go." He gives "thumbs-up" to Ryan and waits for Ryan's signal.

RYAN

returns "thumbs-up."

STRUT

talks into the walkie-talkie.

> STRUT
> Timing sequence ready—
> *(he begins his countdown)*
> 10, 9, 8, — 5, 4, 3, 2, 1, 0—

THE TIMING BUOY

flashes three lights sequentially, red, yellow, then green.

RYAN

flips the "on" switch and suddenly

THE ROCKET BOAT

explodes into motion, the finger-like flame searing the surface of the water as it leaps forward.

THE BOAT

literally flies toward the end of the lake like a missile, hovering several inches above the water as the hydrofoil tynes skim along the water at over 300 mi/hr.

THIS INTERCUT

with Strut, Olivia, the timers, Roger at the finish line, the TV Monitor screens in the TV control van.

RYAN'S POV

The periphery landscape is distorted, flattened as the world plunges into silence and high-speed visual images.

THE BOAT

streaks by as the

(8)

DIGITAL NUMBERS

of the timing mechanisms race toward infinity.

VARIOUS ANGLES

as the boat hurtles toward the finish line. Crew, timers, spectators, watch in breathless wonder.

RYAN

holds onto the steering wheel when suddenly we see his hands "twitch" slightly as the boat vibrates.

TV ANNOUNCER (VO)
It's a solid run—

THE TIMING CONSOLE

The digital numbers spin at a dizzying speed.

RYAN'S POV

The boat shimmies, builds into a pronounced vibration jarring the entire landscape view. Something is terribly wrong.

FROM THE SHORE

We see the rooster tail becoming irregular and choppy.

STRUT AND OLIVIA

watch the boat shaking violently.

A SERIES OF QUICK CUTS

intercut between spectators and boat. Prototype I veers off course, Ryan frozen at the wheel.

> TV ANNOUNCER (VO)
> Wait a minute—something's not—something's wrong—the boat's shaking—

PROTOTYPE I

lists to one side.

RYAN

pushes the eject button.

> TV ANNOUNCER (VO)
> *(hysterical)*
> Ryan can't hold it! Oh, my God! He's crashing—Ryan's crashing—oh, my God—

THE COCKPIT

ejects, arches high into the air, the parachute trailing behind it.

THE CAPSULE

heads toward the water.

STRUT, THE CREW, TIMERS, OLIVIA

watch horrified, disbelieving.

THE BOAT

tips over, smashes into the water, careens out of control, then cartwheels over and over again until it disintegrates before our very eyes.

> TV ANNOUNCER (VO)
> Ryan's ejected—but wait a minute—the chute's
> not opening— Oh, my God—how could this
> happen—what a tragedy!

VARIOUS ANGLES

as the parachute attached to the capsule fails to open. Ryan, encased in the plastic cockpit, hits the water at over 300 mi/hr.

The capsule bounces and skips across the water like a stone on a pond. We can only guess what's happening to Ryan inside. The capsule speeds more than a mile before it finally comes to a stop.

Silence. The world seems frozen in time. And, then:

Ambulance SIRENS shatter the silence, and all hell breaks loose as people move toward the lifeless figure of Jack Ryan floating helplessly in the water. Hold, then:

CUT TO:

Notice how each shot describes the action, and the terms on the list are used to give it a "cinematic" look without resorting to excessive CAMERA instruction.

* * *

As an exercise: Write something in screenplay form. Remember to find the "subject" of the shot. Many times it's helpful to get a screenplay and simply type or write ten pages of it. Any ten pages will do, simply to get the "feel" of writing in screenplay form.

Allow yourself some time to learn how to do it; it may be uncomfortable at first, but it gets easier.

14

Adaptation

*Wherein we approach the art of
adaptation:*

Adapting a novel, book, play, or article into a screenplay is
the same as writing an original screenplay. "To adapt" means
to transpose from one medium to another. *Adaptation* is defined as the ability "to make fit or suitable by changing, or
adjusting"—modifying something to create a change in structure, function, and form, which produces a better adjustment.

Put another way, a novel is a novel, a play a play, a
screenplay a screenplay. Adapting a book into a screenplay
means to change one (a book) into the other (a screenplay),
not superimpose one onto the other. Not a filmed novel or
a filmed stage play. They are two different forms. An apple
and an orange.

When you *adapt* a novel, play, article, or even a song into
a screenplay, you are changing one form into another. You
are writing a screenplay *based on other material.*

In essence, however, you are still writing an original screenplay. And you must approach it the same way.

A novel usually deals with the internal life of someone, the character's thoughts, feelings, emotions, and memories occurring within the *mindscape* of dramatic action. In a novel, you can write the same scene in a sentence, a paragraph, a page, or chapter, describing the internal dialogue, the thoughts, feelings, and impressions of the character. A novel usually takes place inside the character's head.

A play, on the other hand, is told in words, and thoughts, feelings, and events are described in dialogue on a stage locked within the boundaries of the proscenium arch. A play deals with the *language* of dramatic action.

A screenplay deals with *externals,* with details—the ticking of a clock, a child playing in an empty street, a car turning the corner. A screenplay is a story told with pictures, placed within the context of dramatic structure.

Jean-Luc Godard, the innovative French film director who did *Breathless, Weekend,* and *Vivre sa Vie,* says that film is evolving its own language, and that we have to learn how to read the picture.

An adaptation must be viewed as an original screenplay. It only *starts* from the novel, book, play, article, or song. That is *source* material, the starting point. Nothing more.

When you adapt a novel, you are not obligated to remain faithful to the original material.

All the President's Men is a good example. Adapted by William Goldman from the book by Bernstein and Woodward (about Watergate, lest we forget), there were several dramatic choices that had to be made immediately. In an interview at Sherwood Oaks, Goldman says that it was a difficult adaptation. "I had to approach very complicated material in a simple way without making it seem simple-minded. I had to make a story where there wasn't one. It was always a question of trying to figure out what the legitimate story was.

"For example, the movie ends halfway through the book.

We made a decision to end it there, on the Haldeman mistake, rather than show Woodward and Bernstein going on to their greater glory. The audience already knew they had been proven right and gone on and gotten rich and famous and were the media darlings. To try and end *All the President's Men* on an up-beat note would have been a mistake. So we ended it there, on the Haldeman mistake, a little more than halfway through the book. The most important thing about the screenplay was setting up the structure. I had to make sure we found out what we wanted to find out when we wanted to find it out. If the audience is confused, we've lost them."

Goldman opens with the break-in at the Watergate Complex, a taut, suspenseful sequence, and after the capture of the men introduces Woodward (Robert Redford) at the preliminary hearing. He *sees* the high-class attorney in the courtroom, becomes suspicious and then involved. When Bernstein (Dustin Hoffman) joins him on the story (plot point I), they succeed in unraveling the thread of mystery and intrigue that leads to the downfall of the President of the United States.

The original material is source material. What you do with it to fashion it into a screenplay is up to you. You might have to add characters, scenes, incidents, and events. Don't just copy a novel into a screenplay; make it visual, a story told with pictures.

Goldman does this in *Marathon Man*. He adapted his own novel: "People ask me if I wrote it as a screenplay first and I tell them no. Not at all. It was a novel first, and the fact that it was bought for the movies is purely coincidental.

"*Marathon Man* is a very complicated screenplay. The novel is an interior novel; most of the action takes place inside the kid's head. The only scene that plays directly in the book *and* the movie is the scene with Olivier in the diamond district. That is an exterior scene. I didn't have to do very much to it because it always played. It worked in the book, it worked in the screenplay, and it worked on film."

When you adapt a novel into a screenplay you are not obligated to remain true to the original material. Not too long ago I adapted a novel into a screenplay. I had to start from scratch. It was a disaster book about a meteorologist who discovers a new ice age approaching. No one believes him, of course, and when the weather changes it's too late. The new ice age begins. The meteorologist and a group of other scientists are sent to examine the glacier in Iceland, but the ship freezes in the ice. The novel ends with the main character freezing to death.

That was the book. A disaster story of 650 pages that's a downer.

I decided to keep the main character, but I wanted to place him in emotional conflict for more dramatic value. So I made him a politically outspoken professor, who was being considered for tenure at NYU. His "irresponsible" statements about the impending ice age could possibly jeopardize his appointment.

Then I had to figure out what to do about the story. I needed to change the ending into an "upbeat" or positive one. I wanted them to live, not die in the frozen ice. So I had to construct new elements *based* on the novel. I began knowing I wanted an exciting opening. I went through the book and on page 287 found the main character traveling to the glacier in Iceland to measure glacial movement. I decided to open there, on the vast ice plain. A visual element. As they descend deep into the heart of the glacier an earthquake occurs, causing an avalanche. They barely make it out alive. It's a strong, visual sequence and sets up the story appropriately.

When the professor returns to New York and presents his

findings to his superiors, they don't believe him. The first bliz-
zard of the year, the warning, then becomes the plot point
at the end of Act I. It happens on Halloween (my idea) because it's possible and is a good visual sequence.
The shape of things to come.
The second act was another problem. I reduced most of
the action to three major sequences: one, the main character
organizes a world-wide network of scientists to try and solve
the problem; two, New York City freezes; and three, the
people finally accept the truth and try to formulate a plan. I
strung these sequences together with incidents from the book,
knowing I had to avoid all disaster-movie clichés; there was
no market for disaster movies at the time. As mentioned, the
original ending didn't work and had to be changed. I ended
up with a futuristic survival story.

I changed the action so that when the scientist's boat
freezes in the ice (the plot point at the end of Act II), I have
the main character, along with his scientist girl friend and
seven others, leave the boat to try and adapt to conditions of
the ice the way the Eskimos have over the last thousand
years.

Act III, then, is all new. The characters travel in a cell of
nine people, hunting caribou, throwing off the remnants of
the twentieth century. I end the screenplay with the meteorologist's girl friend giving birth to their child.

It worked very well.

When you adapt a novel into a screenplay, it must be a
visual experience. That's your job as screenwriter. You must
remain true only to the *integrity* of the *source material*.

There are exceptions, of course. Perhaps the most unique
exception is the script written by John Huston for *The Maltese Falcon*. Huston had just finished adapting the script of
High Sierra with Humphrey Bogart and Ida Lupino from the
book by W.R. Burnett. The film was very successful, and

Huston was given the opportunity to write and direct his first feature. He decided to remake *The Maltese Falcon* by Dashiell Hammett. The Sam Spade detective story had been filmed twice before by Warner Bros., once as a comedy in 1931, with Ricardo Cortez and Bebe Daniels, and again in 1936, as *Satan Met a Lady* with Warren William and Bette Davis. Both films failed.

Huston liked the feel of the book. He thought he could capture its integrity on film, making it a hard-boiled, gritty detective story in tune with Hammett's style. Just before he left on vacation, he gave the book to his secretary and told her to go through it breaking down the written narrative into screenplay form, labeling each scene as either interior or exterior, and describing the basic action using dialogue from the book. Then he left for Mexico.

While he was away, the script somehow found its way into the hands of Jack L. Warner. "I love it. You've really captured the flavor of this book," he told the startled writer/director. "Shoot it just as it is—with my blessing!"

Huston did just that, and the result is an American film classic.

William Goldman talks about the difficulties he had writing *Butch Cassidy and the Sundance Kid:* "First of all, Western research is dull because most of it's inaccurate. The writers that write Westerns are in the business of perpetuating myths that are false to begin with. It's hard to find out what really happened."

Goldman spent eight years researching Butch Cassidy, and occasionally he would find "a book or some articles or a piece about Butch. There was nothing about Sundance; he was an unknown figure until he went to South America with Butch."

Goldman found it necessary to distort history in order to get Butch and Sundance to leave the country and go to South America. These two outlaws were the last of their breed.

Times were changing, and the Western outlaw could no longer pull the same kind of jobs he'd been doing since the end of the Civil War.

"In the movie," Goldman says, "Butch and Sundance rob some trains, and then a super posse forms and chases them relentlessly. They jump off a cliff when they find out they can't lose them and go to South America. But in real life, when Butch Cassidy heard about the super posse, he took off. He just left. He knew it was the end; he couldn't beat them. . . .

"I felt I had to justify why my hero leaves and runs away, so I tried to make the super posse as implacable as I could so the audience'd be rooting for them to get the hell out of there.

"Most of the movie was made up. I used certain facts. They *did* rob a couple of trains, they *did* take too much dynamite and blow the car to pieces; the same guy Woodcock *was* on both trains, they *did* go to New York, they *did* go to South America, they *did* die in a shoot-out in Bolivia. Other than that, it's all bits and pieces, all made up."

"History," T.S. Eliot once observed, "is but a contrived corridor." If you are writing a historical screenplay, you do not have to be accurate about the people involved, only to the historical event and the result of that event.

If you have to add new scenes, do it. If necessary add a sequence of events that will personalize the story while leading it to an accurate historical result. *Napoleon,* by the French filmmaker Abel Gance, originally made in 1927 and recently excavated by Kevin Brownlow and presented by Francis Ford Coppola, is an extraordinary illustration of how to use history as a springboard. The film traces Napoleon's early life (Gance dramatizes the child's remarkable military ability in a snowfight. Action is character, remember!), and then jumps to 1789 to show six years of the French Revolution, ending with Napoleon assuming command of the French

Army. The film ends with the magnificent triptych sequence (a three-screen process) where Napoleon leads the French Army into Italy.

Don't be *too* free with history, however.

In a recent European screenwriting workshop, a French student wrote a film about Napoleon being transported from Waterloo to St. Helena. He made it into a romantic swashbuckler, an action-adventure story filled with historical inaccuracies and blatantly fictitious events. He failed to prepare or research his story sufficiently for it to be anything but a good example of bad writing.

Adapting a play into a screenplay must be approached in the same manner. You're dealing with a different *form* but utilizing the same principles.

A play is told through dialogue and deals with the *language* of dramatic action. Characters talk about how they feel, about memories, emotions, events. Talking heads. The stage, the sets, the background, are forever fixed within the restrictions of the proscenium arch.

There was a time in Shakespeare's career when he cursed the restrictions of the stage, calling it "an unworthy scaffold" and "this wooden *O*," and begged the audience to "eke out the performance with your mind." He knew the stage couldn't capture the vast spectacle of two armies stationed against an empty sky on the rolling plains of England. Only when he completed *Hamlet* did he transcend the limitations of the stage and create great stage art.

When you adapt a play into a screenplay, you've got to visualize events that are referred to or spoken about. Plays deal with language and dramatic dialogue. In *Streetcar Named Desire* or *Cat on a Hot Tin Roof* by Tennessee Williams, Arthur Miller's *Death of a Salesman,* or Eugene O'Neill's *Long Day's Journey Into Night,* the action takes place on stage, in sets, the actors talking to themselves or each other. Take a look at any play, whether it be a contemporary play by Sam Shepard like *Curse of the Starving Class,* or Edward Albee's *Who's Afraid of Virginia Woolf.*

Because the action of a play is spoken, you've got to open it up to add a visual dimension. You might have to add scenes and dialogue that are only referred to in the text, then structure, design, and write them in such a way that they lead you into the main scenes that occur on stage. Search the dialogue for ways to expand the action visually.

A good example is the Australian film *Breaker Morant.* The play, written by Kenneth Ross (who wrote *Day of the Jackal*), then adapted and directed by the Australian filmmaker Bruce Beresford, tells the story of an Australian military commando who is accused, court-martialed, and finally executed for killing the enemy in "an unorthodox and uncivilized fashion" (guerrilla warfare) during the Boer War (1900). He becomes a political victim, a pawn in the game of war, an Australian sacrifice to the English Colonial system at the turn of the century. The play takes place in the courtroom, but the film opens the action to include flashbacks of battles as well as scenes from the soldier's personal life. The result is a stunning and thought-provoking film.

Play and film stand on their own, a tribute to both playwright and filmmaker.

Screenplays dealing with people, either alive or dead— biographical scripts—must be selective and focused in order to be effective. *Young Winston,* for example, written by Carl Foreman, deals with only a few incidents in the life of Winston Churchill before he was elected Prime Minister.

Your character's life is only the beginning. Be selective! Choose only a few incidents or events from your character's life, then structure them into a dramatic story line. *Coal*

Miner's Daughter by Tom Rickman, *Lawrence of Arabia* written by Robert Bolt, and *Citizen Kane* (loosely adapted from the life of William Randolph Hearst) by Orson Welles and Herman Mankiewicz, are good examples of a few incidents in a character's life laid out and structured in dramatic fashion.

How you approach your subject's life determines the basic story line: without a story line you've got no story; without a story you've got no screenplay.

A short time ago, one of my students obtained the motion-picture rights to the life of the first woman editor on a major metropolitan newspaper. She tried to get everything into the story—the early years "because they were *so* interesting"; her marriage and children "because she had such an unusual approach"; her early years as a reporter when she covered several major stories "because they were *so* exciting"; and getting the job of editor and several stories because "that's what she's famous for."

I tried to convince her to focus only on a few events in the woman's life, but she was too tied into the subject to see anything objectively. So I gave her an exercise. I told her to write her story line in a few pages. She came back with 26 pages and was only halfway through her character's life! She didn't have a story, she had a chronology, and it was boring. I told her it wasn't working, and suggested she focus on one or two of the stories in the editor's career. A week later, she came back saying she had been unable to choose which ones were the right ones. Overwhelmed by indecision, she became despondent and depressed and finally gave up in despair. She called me one day in tears, and I urged her to get back into the material, to choose three of the most interesting events in the woman's life (writing, remember, *is* choice and selection), and if need be, to talk to the woman about what *she* thought were the most interesting aspects of *her* life and career. She did and managed to create a story line based on the newspaper story she covered that led to her appointment as the first woman editor. It became the "hook" or basis of the screenplay.

You only have 120 pages to tell your story. Choose your events carefully so they highlight and illustrate your script with good visual and dramatic components. The screenplay should be based on the dramatic needs of your story. Source material *is*, after all, source material. It is a starting point, not an end in itself.

Journalists seem to have a hard time learning this. They often have a difficult time with a screenplay based on an article. I don't know why, except perhaps that the methods of constructing a dramatic story line in film are exactly the opposite of those in journalism.

A journalist approaches his/her assignment by getting facts and gathering information, by doing text research as well as interviewing people related to the piece. Once they have all the facts, they can figure out the story. The more facts a journalist can collect, the more information he has; he can use some, all, or none of it. Once he's collected the facts, he searches for the "hook" or "angle" of the piece, and then writes the story using only those facts that highlight and support the material.

That's good journalism.

But writing a screenplay is exactly the opposite. You approach a script with an *idea,* a *subject,* an action and character, then weave a story line that will dramatize it. Once you have the basic story line—three guys holding up the Chase Manhattan Bank—you expand it; you do research, create characters, do character biographies, interview people if need be, collect all the missing facts and information that build and support your story. If you need something for the story, make it up!

The facts *support* the story in a screenplay; you might even say they create the story.

In screenwriting, you go from general to specific; you find the story first, then collect facts. In journalism, you go from specific to general; you collect the facts first, then find the story.

A well-known journalist was writing a screenplay based on a controversial article he had written for a national magazine. All the facts were at his disposal, yet he found it extremely difficult to let go of the article and dramatize the elements he needed to make it a good screenplay. He got stuck in finding the "right" facts and the "right" details, and then couldn't get beyond the first 30 pages of the screenplay. He bogged down, went into a panic, then shelved what might have been a very good screenplay.

He couldn't let the article be the article and the screenplay the screenplay. He wanted to be faithful to the other material, and it just doesn't work.

Many people want to write a screenplay or teleplay based on a magazine or newspaper article. If you're going to adapt an article into a screenplay, you've got to approach it from a screenwriter's point of view. What's the story about? Who's the main character? What's the ending? Is it about a man who was captured, tried, and then acquitted for murder only to discover after the trial that he was really guilty? Is it about a young man who designs, builds, and races cars and becomes a champion? About a doctor finding a cure for diabetes? About incest? *Who* is it about? *What* is it about? When you answer those questions, you can lay it out in dramatic structure.

There are many legal problems if you adapt a screenplay or teleplay from an article or story. First of all, you must obtain permission to write a script: that means getting the rights from the people involved, negotiating with the author, and possibly with the magazine or newspaper. Most people are willing to cooperate in trying to bring their stories to the screen or TV. An entertainment attorney who specializes in these matters, or a literary agent, should be consulted if you're serious.

Don't get bogged down with the legalities, however. If you don't want to deal with it now, don't deal with it. Write the script or outline first. Something attracted you to the material. What is it? Explore it. You might decide to write the script based on the article or story and then see how it turns out. If it's good, you may want to show it to the people involved. If you *don't do it,* you'll never know how it would have turned out. And that's what it's all about.

We've discussed adapting novels, plays, and articles into screenplays, and still the question must be asked: What *is* the fine art of adaptation?

Answer: NOT being true to the original. A book is a book, a play a play, an article an article, a screenplay a screenplay. An adaptation is always an original screenplay. They are different forms.

Just like apples and oranges.

*   *   *

As an exercise: Open a novel at random and read a few pages. Notice how the narrative action is described. Does it take place inside the character's head? Is it told with dialogue? What about description? Take a play and do the same thing. Notice how the characters talk about themselves or the action of the play. Talking heads. Then read a few pages of a screenplay (any that are excerpted in this text will do) and notice how the screenplay deals with *external* details and events, what the character *sees*.

15

Writing with Computers

Wherein we discuss the agony and the ecstasy:

When I talk about writing the screenplay on computer, many writer friends of mine who have not made the transition from typewriter to word processor just freak out. As intelligent and professional as they are, when they confront the idea, or the possibility, of changing their writing habits, their writing instrument, they just can't deal with it. They shake their heads, shrug their shoulders, smile, and boldly declare that no, they're not into that. They'd rather continue the way of writing that's comfortable and familiar to them even if it means hours and hours of tedious and laborious work, of typing and cutting and pasting, of transcribing arrows, and illegible words, of hoping your typist can decipher everything, and then hoping he or she doesn't lose the pages because you gave them the original and you don't have any copy or backup.

I certainly understand that. I felt the same way when I started thinking about giving up one way of writing for another. It's tough.

I say that now, because for the past several years I've been writing on a computer. Like most of the people I know,

I fought it for a while, refusing to get hooked by the "new technology." But I certainly thought about it, contemplated it, discussed it, and then, in the end, dismissed it.

I simply didn't want to change my writing experience. I thought that if I changed the way I wrote, it would somehow inhibit the creative process. I was also afraid of learning the new computer technology.

For many years I had been writing on a typewriter, first a manual, then an electric. I changed my work habits once, after a few years' hiatus, when I started writing in longhand on legal tablets before I typed everything up. I was satisfied. Everything was fine.

But as computer technology continued to evolve, I kept hearing how easy it was writing on computer, how it was a freeing, liberating experience. For those who didn't know how to type, there were typing programs that could teach them to type and learn the computer simultaneously. Typing should never get in the way of writing.

Once I heard one of my students talking about the joys of writing with a computer. When I asked why he liked it so much, he told me that when he was writing on a computer he "was writing 100 percent of the time," but that when he was writing on the typewriter, he was writing only about 25 percent of the time; the rest of the time he was "retyping."

That made a lot of sense to me. I was writing my first "words on pages" in longhand, then would type the pages, edit in longhand, retype, re-edit, retype, and so on. This student suddenly made me aware of the *work* of writing. So I started looking at how much writing I was doing, compared to how much work, or typing, I was doing.

I began observing my work habits, and soon became aware that I was spending about 30 percent writing and about 70 percent typing. I don't like typing, I like writing. There had to be a better way. Maybe the computer was it.

So I seriously started exploring the world of computers. I knew nothing about it, so I talked to friends, read ads in the papers, talked to people, and went to huge chain stores, which drove me crazy because the salespeople weren't interesting in explaining their product, they only wanted to know what I wanted. I didn't know what I wanted. I didn't know whether I should build my writing system around hardware or software, whether I should get an IBM or a Macintosh, whether hard disk or dual drive, or whether I wanted Microsoft Word as my word processing unit, or WordPerfect, or maybe Wordstar, or any of the other word processing systems on the market.

What I wanted was a computer, but that meant I needed the many component parts that make up a computer: the CPU (the guts of the system); the monitor, or screen; a printer to print everything out, the "hard copy." I also found I needed a word processing system, the software; the backup or "floppy" disks; and, to ensure everything doesn't blow out of the wall, a surge protector.

My needs were simple, but I was totally confused. I just wanted to sit down and write on a computer. Soon, I began looking for someone who could make my head stop spinning. I needed someone who could put everything together, tell me what I needed, based on what I could afford to pay and the way I work. Without such guidance, I was sinking fast in the quicksand of indecision.

I finally found a store that specializes in writers who write with computers, The Writer's Computer Store in West Los Angeles and Sausalito, California, and let them make the major decisions for me: hardware, hard disk, word processing program, all of it.

The first choice I had to deal with was the hardware; IBM, or IBM-compatible, or the Apple-Macintosh. Both use different systems, and when you buy a computer you may need to purchase a unit that is compatible with the computer of another person if you're working with a partner. IBM or IBM-compatible to IBM-compatible, and Macintosh to Macintosh. In a few years they will be compatible with each other, but now you have to go through another system to translate IBM language into Macintosh language. It's a drag.

The Mac is certainly easy to use, especially the new Powerbook, and without question almost every writer who works with it absolutely loves it. When I was buying my equipment, the Writer's Computer Store did not carry the Macintosh line, neither hardware nor software (they carry both lines now), so I ended up getting an IBM-compatible with a hard-disk drive. (Hard disk is the only way to go, and I love it.) However, both systems are very good and very usable. It really doesn't make any difference which system you choose.

Three things should govern your choice. Price, of course, is the first. Second: The unit must do what you want it to do. The third thing, and for me perhaps the most important, is that you have someone to turn to if the computer goes down. And it will go down, no matter what unit you get. The most important decision I made was buying my computer at a store where I could call for help and someone would be there to guide me through. That's very important. I can't tell you how many times I've called the Writer's Computer Store for help, and they would guide me out of a perilous panic.

Another word of advice: If you buy a computer, the kids should *not* be using it. Period. The computer is for you; treat it like a musician treats his instrument.

The next decision I had to make was the word processing system; the two most popular are Microsoft Word, and WordPerfect. Both are competent, and both are easy to use once you learn the system. I use Microsoft Word because I was trained on it, and now, using Microsoft Word for Windows, I can actually do graphics right on the screen: titles, chapter headings, charts, graphs, or highlighting special words or headings.

At this writing, WordPerfect has just come out with a new version, 6.0, which offers specialized features but takes up a lot of space on the hard disk; they all do. The 6.0 version can do a full spreadsheet and has a good file management system, as well as program launching and switching. The writing tools are strong, and you can do graphics with it as well.

The new Microsoft Word (6.0) also offers a large selection of features: AutoCorrect allows you to correct spelling mistakes automatically, as well as look for common mistakes we all make, such as not capitalizing the first word of a sentence, or accidentally starting a word with two capitals. This is an optional part of the word processing program, and you can either use it or not; it's your call. This version also allows you to do in-place editing and import elements from other programs. There are many other features as well. It's a whole new way of working with computers. Windows is the future.

Both systems are very good and state-of-the-art, but there are a lot of professional computer people who do not want to deal with WordPerfect 6.0. They say the program is slow executing commands, so make sure you checkout the program before you buy it.

As far as monitors and printers go, there are so many types and brands on the market that you have to be guided by your wallet and your needs. I want my pages to be letter perfect, so I chose a laser printer. The new models are quiet, print about eight copies a minute, and the page looks beautiful. They're more money, but they're worth it. Shop around, see the differences among each of the models and brands, and check the prices carefully. It's a competitive market.

The same goes for monitors. The monitor you want can

be color or not, although most of the new programs being created for the marketplace require a color monitor. The only difference is price.

There's one more variable: the mouse. The mouse is a small, portable, hand-held control indicator; it allows you to perform many necessary computer functions quickly and easily. I can't write without a mouse, yet many friends of mine can't use it at all. Some of the new, smaller computers, such as the Powerbook, have a mouse built right into the unit. The new Windows environment, either for IBM or Mac, requires a mouse. Your choice will depend solely on personal preference.

Writing a screenplay on computer poses a unique set of problems for a writer. Number one, screenplay form is so complicated that a number of screenwriting programs have been created simply to deal with formatting, page breaks, slug lines, margins, all the "mores" and "continueds" you need to connect the dialogue and description from scene to scene and page to page.

The most important question you have to ask yourself is whether to get a dedicated screenwriting program, or whether to add a formatting option to your existing word processing program.

STAND-ALONE PROGRAMS

At this writing there are a couple of very good stand-alone script processing programs for screenwriters; if you are a Macintosh user, perhaps the most popular is Final Draft. Designed to combine the writing and the formatting into one complete system, Final Draft is a dedicated screenwriting processing program that incorporates all the formatting rules that make screenwriting unique: preset margins, built-in character lists, scene numbers, page breaks, and automatic pagination. All you have to do is write the script. There's even a "Scriptnote" section where you can leave notes for yourself in a scene or sequence, move on, and then come back later to do the rewriting.

For IBM and IBM-compatible users, the best and most popular dedicated script writing program at this writing is Scriptware. It's simple and easy to use because it is based on typewriter keys. Pressing the Tab and Enter keys takes you where you want to go. The program features margins, automatically capitalizes character names, inserts scene numbers, and automatically inserts page breaks while you are writing. What you see on the screen is the exact way it looks on the page. You can also make notes to yourself anywhere in the text; Scriptware totally supports the writer through the screenwriting process.

In the very near future there will be many stand-alone screenwriting programs. The first of the popular programs was MovieMaster, but it has no mouse support; a new upgraded Version 4 is now on the market.

ADD-ONS

If you're fluent in any of the three major word processing programs—Microsoft Word for DOS, Word for Windows, or WordPerfect for DOS—you may simply want to "add on" a screenwriting program. Warren Script Applications (MS Word for DOS, or Windows) takes you from start to finish fairly easily, with simple keystrokes for character names, dialogue, and sluglines. It also processes scripts for production needs and makes revisions and shot lists. This is done only with MS Word, so if you're already using Word, there's not much you have to learn. There's also a Warren Script Applications for Word for Windows 2.0 that incorporates all formats.

For WordPerfect 5.1 users, there is Script Perfection and SuperScript Pro. Script Perfection uses pull-down menus and formats for both screenplays and sitcoms. SuperScript Pro for 5.1 records frequently used character names by letter and even types them. So does Script Perfection, though the difference between them is that the user no longer has to split the script into three segments (documents). The new version handles the available memory of the computer more efficiently though it requires a minimum of two MB. Other features have been added as well, but there is still no mouse support. It processes the script with scene numbers and "mores" and "continueds" on the top and bottom of the pages, as do most of the other programs. It also includes formats for TV sitcom and the stage. SuperScript for WordPerfect 5.0 and 5.1 is a program for people who have not upgraded their WordPerfect program.

Then there is Scriptor, one of the industry's first feature script formatting programs. Scriptor works with many word processing programs and performs the functions of a page breaking program, including script numbers, dialogue breaks, and revision marks. It's a good program, but its real function is not performed until after the script has been written. But it is a very good program for script breakdowns, and is quite popular with the production people in the film industry.

IDEA GENERATORS

What about a program that inspires the screenwriter with ideas and story guidance? Is there such an animal? There are a couple of "idea generators" that claim to help stimulate your creativity. Most notable at this time are the IdeaFisher program and Plots Unlimited. IdeaFisher claims to allow you to expand your ideas through "a proven, focused process of association.'' It provides questions and answers and associations, supposedly to help you to clarify and define your story.

Plots Unlimited is a program that suggests many, many plot, subplot, and character combinations. You can start with the MasterPlot or the Character Generation feature, and you can quickly access some thirteen thousand plot possibilities and eighteen hundred conflict situations. At least that's what the literature claims. It also says it's "a MUST" for anyone working in episodic TV. I don't know whether that's true, and I'm always a little skeptical about the claims of these types of programs.

STRUCTURE AND STORY GUIDANCE

What the makers of these programs claim and what the programs do are two different things. Collaborator is a simple series of questions that the makers say helps you produce a story outline with characters, locations, plot complications, crises, and resolution. I would like to believe the PR. I find the program to be somewhat thin and elementary in building and structuring the story line.

The makers of Final Draft have just developed the new Corkboard program for Macintosh that uses the concept of index cards to help organize your ideas. It allows you to structure, categorize, sort, and view any scenes, characters, plot, or story ideas easily and succinctly. It can be used for a screenplay, a play, or a novel. It has been designed to be used with Final Draft but the makers tell me it can also be used independently.

OTHER PROGRAMS THAT MIGHT BE USEFUL

Several other programs are available that might be useful for writing the screenplay on computer. One of those is Write

Pro; the literature claims you can "create rounded characters, develop heroes and villains, set up dramatic conflicts, and expand the dimensions of plot." The eight lessons were developed by a writer, and are not interactive.

Another program is called FirstAid for Writers, which works for fiction and nonfiction writers. Some of the title headings of the program sound good but seem very thin: "Gearing-Up," the brochure says, "jump-starts your imagination; QuickFix examines the first-sentence dilemma, examines plotting, creates tension, suspense, and place; Intervention, Nonfiction, and Refresher are other segments." I don't use programs like this so I don't know whether the PR blurb is accurate and really helps you do the job. Check it out before you jump in and purchase it. That goes for everything you're thinking of buying.

There are other film programs available as well, things such as RightWriter, or Gram.mat.ik, which don't work well for screenwriting because there are no "rules" for dialogue; and there's even a Random House Encyclopedia; then there's something called The Writer's Toolkit. There are a lot of other film programs on the market that are specifically designed for the needs of film production: software for scheduling, budgeting, production boards, credits, movie guides, and more. There's even an interactive movie guide on CD ROM called Cinemania, and a Storyboard Quick program.

In the near future, with the interactive market becoming so predominant, there will be more and more computer-generated software created for the expanding screenwriting market. Industry experts are predicting more than five hundred channels will be created for this "information super-highway" of new technology. "Terminator 2: Judgment Day," (James Cameron and William Wisher) and "Jurassic Park," (David Koepp) have revolutionized the movie industry and the explosion of computer-generated graphics will probably proliferate into the interactive field of programming. And it's not going to stop there. The decade of the '90s will see advances in the scientific computer technology that defy speculation, so hang on—it's going to a "bumpy ride."

Some of these new type computer applications, like the CD ROM environment, are still in their infancy. People are talking about "nonlinear" stories for the new interactive field, and some software has just come on the market that is designed for this nonlinear story construction. One such program is called StoryVision and allows you to select certain key scenes that will help build your story. This nonlinear approach to storytelling has led to a lot of discussion and experimentation, but I don't really think it will help the majority of people writing. Story is story, and must be built on a firm foundation. If there is any "rule" about writing, it is that *story determines structure; structure does not determine story.*

If you've made the decision to write with computer, the only valid principle to follow is to determine what you need, not what you want. Hunting through the numerous computer stores for something to help get you started, or something to help you understand the dynamics of screenwriting, *be careful*! The market will soon be flooded with claims guaranteed to tell you what to do, and how to do it.

If only it were true.

When you get right down to it, you're the one who's going to be facing the blank computer screen. Most of us have a tendency to look outside ourselves for help, whether in the form of a teacher, a book, a class, a tool, or some other kind of aid. Some are very important to investigate and explore, simply to sharpen your screenwriting skills. But the truth is that everything you need, all the resources you're looking for to help and guide and support you, are all there right inside you.

Screenwriting software will help you write, but it won't tell you *what* to write, or *how* to write it. No matter what guidance you seek, what help you get, it always comes back to you.

For you are your own teacher.

16

On Collaboration

Wherein we approach methods of collaboration:

While I was attending the University of California at Berkeley, I had the privilege of working with Jean Renoir, the great French film director. It was an extraordinary experience. Son of the great painter Auguste Renoir and creator of two of the greatest films ever made, *Grand Illusion* and *Rules of the Game*, Renoir was a man who loved film with religious passion.

He loved to talk, and we loved listening to him for hours on end, talking about the relationship between art and film. Because of his background and tradition, Renoir felt that film, though a great art, was not a "true" art in the sense that writing, painting, or music is, because too many people are directly involved in its making. The filmmaker can write, direct, and produce his own film, Renoir used to say, but he can't act all the parts; he can be the cameraman (Renoir loved to paint with light), but he can't develop the film. He sends it to a special film laboratory for that, and sometimes it doesn't come back the way he wants it.

"One person can't do everything," Renoir used to say. "True art is in the *doing* of it."

Renoir was right. Film is a collaborative medium. The filmmaker depends on others to bring his vision to the screen. The technical skills required to make a movie are extremely specialized. And the state of the art is constantly improving. The only thing you can do by yourself is write a screenplay. All you need is pen and paper, or a typewriter or computer, and a certain amount of time. You can write it alone or with someone.

It's your choice.

Screenwriters collaborate all the time. If a producer has an idea and commissions you to write it, you will be in a collaboration with the producer and director. In *Raiders of the Lost Ark,* for example, Lawrence Kasdan, the screenwriter *(The Empire Strikes Back,* writer/director of *Body Heat),* met with George Lucas and Steven Spielberg. Lucas wanted to use the name of his dog, Indiana Jones, for the hero (Harrison Ford), and he knew what the last scene of the movie would be: a vast military basement warehouse filled with thousands of crates of confiscated secrets, much like *Citizen Kane*'s basement was filled with huge crates of art. That's all Lucas knew about *Raiders* at the time. Spielberg wanted to add a mystical dimension. They spent two weeks locked in an office, and when the three of them emerged, they had worked out a general story line. Then Lucas and Spielberg left to work on other projects, and Kasdan went into his office and wrote *Raiders of the Lost Ark.*

That's a typical collaboration in Hollywood. Everybody works for the finished product.

Writers collaborate for different reasons. Some think it's easier to work with someone else. Most comedy writers work in teams, especially television writers, and shows like *Saturday Night Live* have a staff of five or ten writers working on each episode. A comedy writer has to be both gag man and audience—a laugh is a laugh. Only the gifted few like Woody Allen or Neil Simon can sit in a room alone and know what's funny and what isn't.

There are three basic stages in the collaborative process. One, establishing the ground rules of the collaboration; two, the preparation needed to write the screenplay; and three, the actual writing itself. All three are essential. If you decide to collaborate, you better go into it with your eyes open. For example, do you like your potential collaborator? You're going to be working with that person for several hours a day for many months, so you had better enjoy being with him or her. Otherwise, you're starting off with problems.

Collaboration is a relationship. It's a fifty-fifty proposition. Two or more people are working together to create an end product, a screenplay. That's the aim, goal, and purpose of your collaboration, and that's where all your energy should be directed. Collaborators tend to lose sight of that very quickly.

They get bogged down in "being right" and various ego struggles, so it's best you ask yourself some questions first. For example, why are *you* collaborating? Why is your *partner* collaborating? What's the reason you're choosing to work with somebody else? Because it's easier? Safer? Not as lonely?

What do you think collaborating with someone on a screenplay looks like? Most people have a picture of one person sitting at a desk in front of a typewriter, typing like crazy, while his partner paces the room rapidly, snapping out words and phrases like a chef preparing a meal. You know, a "writing team." A talker and a typist.

Is that the way you see it? It may have been that way at one time, during the twenties and thirties with writing teams like Moss Hart and George S. Kaufman, but it's not that way anymore.

Everyone works differently. We all have our own style, our own pace, our own likes and dislikes. I think the best example of a collaboration is the musical collaboration between Elton John and Bernie Taupen. At the height of their fame, Bernie Taupen would write a set of lyrics, then mail them to Elton John, somewhere in the world who would then lay down the music, arrange it, and finally record it.

That's the exception, not the rule.

If you want to collaborate, you must be willing to find the right way to work—the right style, the right methods, the right working procedure. Try different things out, make mistakes, go through the collaborative process by trial and error until you find the best way for you and your partner. "The sequences tried that *don't* work," my film-editor friend said, "are the ones that show you what *does* work."

There are no rules when it comes to collaboration. You get to create them, to make them up as you go along. Just like a marriage. You've got to create it, sustain it, and maintain it. You're dealing with someone else all the time. Collaboration is a fifty-fifty proposition with an equal division of labor.

There are four basic positions in collaboration: writer, researcher, typist, and editor. No position is *more* equal than another.

What does your collaboration look like to *you* and *your partner*? What are your goals? Your expectations? What do *you* see yourself doing in the collaboration? What is *your partner* going to do?

Open up a dialogue. Who's going to do the typing? Where are you going to work? When? Who's going to do what?

Talk about it. Discuss it.

Lay down the ground rules. What's the division of labor? You might list the things that have to be done, two or three trips to the library, three, possibly more, interviews. Organize and divide up the tasks. I like to do this, so I'll do this, you do that, and so on. Do things you like to do. If you like to use the library, do it; if your partner likes to interview people, let him do it. It's all part of the writing process.

What does the work schedule look like? Do you have full-time jobs? When are you going to get together? Where? Make sure it's convenient for both of you. If you have a job or a family or are in a relationship, sometimes it gets difficult. Deal with it.

Are you a morning person, an afternoon person, or an evening person? That is, do you work the best in the morning, the afternoon, or the evening? If you don't know, try it one way and see what happens. If it's working, stay with it. If not, try it another way. See what works best for both of you. Support each other. You're both working for the same thing, the completed screenplay.

You'll need a couple of weeks simply to explore and organize a work schedule that supports both of you.

Don't be afraid to try something that doesn't work. Go for it! Make mistakes. Create your collaboration by trial and error. And don't plan on doing any serious writing until the ground rules are set.

The last thing you're going to do is write.

Before you can do that, you've got to prepare the material.

What kind of story are you writing? Is it going to be an action-adventure story with a strong love interest or a love story with a strong action-adventure interest? You better find out. Is it a contemporary story or a historical story? Is it a period piece? What do you have to do to research it? Spend one or two days at the library or several days? Do you have to interview any people? Or sit in on a legal proceeding? And then—who's going to type it up?

Collaboration is a fifty-fifty division of labor.

Who's going to do what?

Talk about it. Work it out. What do you *like* to do? What do you do *best?* Do you like collecting facts and data and then organizing them for background material? Do you work best talking or writing? Find out. If you don't like it, you can always change it.

The same thing with the story. Work on the story together. Verbalize the story line in a few sentences. What is the subject of your story? What's the action? Who's the main character? What's it about? Is your story about an archeologist assigned to recover the lost Ark just before World War II? Who is your main character? What is the dramatic need of your character?

Write the character biographies. You may want to talk about each character with your collaborator, and then write one biography while your partner writes another. Or you may write the biographies, and your collaborator edit them. Know your characters. Talk about them, about who they are and where they come from. Feed the pot. The more you put in, the more you can take out.

After you do the character work, structure the story line. What's the ending, the resolution of your story? Do you know the opening? The plot points at the end of Acts I and II?

If you don't, who does?

Lay your story out so you know where you're going. When you know your ending, the opening, and the two plot points, you're ready to expand your story line in a scene progression using 3 × 5 cards. Discuss it. Talk about it. Argue about it. Just make sure you know your story. You may agree or disagree about it. You may want it one way, your partner another. If you can't resolve it, write it both ways. See which works the best. Work toward the finished product, the screenplay.

It's possible to spend anywhere from three to six weeks or more preparing your material—the research, the characters, building a story line, and creating the mechanics of your collaboration. It's an interesting experience because you're building another kind of relationship. Magic at times, hell at others.

When you're ready to write, things sometimes get crazy. Be prepared. How are you going to put it down on paper? What are the mechanics involved? Who says what, and why is that word better than this word? Who says so? *I'm* right and you're wrong is one point of view. The other point of view, of course, is You're wrong and I'm right!

Collaboration means working together.

The key to collaboration, or any relationship, is communication. You've got to talk to each other. Without communication, there's no collaboration. Only misunderstanding and disagreement. That's nowhere. You two are working together to write and complete a screenplay. There will be times when you'll want to chuck it and walk away. You might think it's not worth it. You may be right. Usually, it's just some of your psychological "stuff" coming up. You know, all the stuff we have to contend with on a day-to-day basis, the fears, insecurities, guilts, judgments, and so on. Deal with it! Writing is learning more about yourself. Be willing to make mistakes, to learn from each other what is working and what isn't.

There are many ways of working, and you're going to have to find your own way. You may work together, with one of you sitting at the typewriter or pad, and the two of you laying out words and ideas. This works well for some people. You will agree on some things, disagree on others; you win some, you lose some. It's a good opportunity to learn about negotiation and compromise in a working relationship.

Another method is to work in 30-page units. You write Act

I, and your partner edits it. Your partner writes Act II, and you edit it. You write Act III, and your partner edits it. This way you see what your partner is writing and can act as editor.

When I work in a collaboration, we both decide upon story and characters. When the preliminary work is done, we work in 30-page units. My collaborator will write Act I. We'll talk by phone to handle any problems that might arise.

When the first act is done, a fairly tight and clean words-on-paper draft, I read and edit it. Is it working? Do we need another scene here? Does the dialogue have to be clarified? Expanded? Sharpened? Is the dramatic premise clearly staged? By words and picture? Are we setting it up properly? I may add some lines or a scene here and there, and occasionally sketch in certain visual aspects.

Sometimes you have to criticize your partner's work. How are you going to tell him that his writing is terrible, that he better throw it away and start over! You better think about what you're going to say. Realize you're dealing with your partner's feelings based on your *judgments*. "Judge not lest ye be judged." You've got to respect and support (hopefully) the other person. First determine *what* you want to say, then decide *how* to say it the best. If you want to say something, say it to yourself first. How would you feel if your partner told you what you're going to tell him?

Collaboration is a learning experience.

Sometimes changes have to be made in Act I before moving on to Act II. The process is exactly the same. Writing is writing. Bring the material to a semirough stage, then move on. You can always polish it. Don't worry about making your pages perfect. You're going to change it anyway, so don't worry about how good it is. It may not be very good. So what? Just get it down, then you can work on it to make it better.

Once you complete the first words-on-paper stage, go back and read it. See what you've got. You should be able to see it as a whole and obtain some kind of overview or perspective on the material. You might need to add some new scenes, create a new character, possibly telescope two scenes into one. Do it!

It's all part of the writing process.

If you're married and want to collaborate with your spouse, other factors are involved. When things get difficult, for example, you simply can't walk away from the collaboration. It's part of the marriage. If the marriage is in trouble, your collaboration will only magnify what's wrong with it. You can't be an ostrich and pretend it isn't there. You've got to deal with it.

For example, some married friends of mine, both professional journalists, decided to write a screenplay together. At the time, she was in between assignments and he was in the middle of one.

She had time on her hands, so she decided to get a head start and began the research. She went to the library, read books, interviewed people, then typed up the material. She didn't mind because "someone's got to do it!"

He had completed his assignment by the time the research was done. They took a few days off, then got down to work. The first thing he said was "Let's see what you've got." Then he proceeded to appraise the material as if it were *his* assignment and the work had been done by a researcher, not his collaborator, not his wife! She was angry, but said nothing. She had done *all* the work, and now he was going to come in and *save* the project!

That's how it began. It got worse. They didn't talk about *how* they were going to work together, only that they *would* work together. No ground rules were established, no decisions made about who does what or when, and no work schedule has been set up.

She works in the morning and writes fast, throwing words down quickly with lots of blank spaces, then goes back and rewrites three or four times until it's right. He works at night, writing slowly, crafting each word and phrase with delicate precision; the first draft is almost a final one.

When they began working together they had no idea about what to expect from each other. She had collaborated once before, but he never had. They both had expectations about what the other would do, but didn't communicate them to each other.

They set up their schedule so she would write the first act—that was the material she had researched—and he would write Act II.

She got down to work. She was a little insecure—it was her *first* screenplay—and she worked hard to overcome the form and resistance. She wrote the first ten pages, then asked him to read them. She didn't know if she was on the right track or not. Was she setting up the story correctly? Was it what they had discussed and talked about? Were the characters real people in real situations? Her concern was natural.

He was working on the second scene of Act II when she gave him the first ten pages. He didn't want to look at them because he was having *his* problems and was just beginning to find his style. The scene was a difficult one; and he'd been working on it for several days.

He took the pages, then put them aside and went back to work, saying nothing to his wife. She gave him a few days to read the material. When he didn't read it, she became angry, so he promised he would read them that night. That satisfied her, at least for the moment.

She got up early the next morning. He was still sleeping

having worked late the night before. She made coffee and tried to work for a while. But it was no use. She wanted to know what her husband, her "collaborator," thought about the pages she had written. What was taking him so long?

The more she thought about it, the more impatient she became. She had to know. Finally, she made a decision; what he didn't know wouldn't hurt him. Quietly she crept into his office and softly closed the door behind her.

She went to his desk and started rifling his papers to see what comments, if any, he had made on her first ten pages. She finally found them, but there was nothing on them—no marks, no comments, no nothing. He didn't read them! Angry, she started to read his pages to see what he was so hung up about.

That's when she heard the noise on the stairs. The door suddenly burst open, and her husband stood framed in the doorway, yelling, "Get away from that desk!" She tried to explain, but he didn't listen. He accused her of spying, of meddling, of invading his privacy. She erupted, and all the anger and tension and withheld communication came pouring out. They went at it, fighting tooth and nail, no holds barred. It *all* came out; resentment, frustration, fear, anxiety, insecurity. It was a screaming match. Even the dog started barking. At the peak of their "collaboration" he picked her up bodily, dragged her across the floor, and literally threw her out of the office, slamming the door in her face. She took off her shoe and stood there pounding on the door. Her heel marks are still etched into his office door.

Now they can laugh about it.

It wasn't funny then. They didn't speak for days.

They learned a great deal from the experience. They learned that fighting doesn't work in a collaboration. They learned to work together and communicate on a more personal and professional level. They learned to criticize each other in a positive and supportive way without fear and restraint. They learned to respect each other. They learned that every person has a right to his or her own writing style, and you can't change it, only support it. She learned to respect the way he styles and fashions words into polished prose. He learned to admire and respect the way she works—fast, clean, and accurate, always getting the job done. They learned how to ask for help from each other, something that was difficult for both of them. They learned from each other.

When they completed the screenplay, they felt a sense of satisfaction and achievement in what they had accomplished.

Collaboration means "working together."

That's what it's all about.

∗   ∗   ∗

As an exercise: If you decide to collaborate, design the writing experience into three stages: the ground rules, the preparation, and the mechanics of writing the material.

17

After It's Written

Wherein we discuss what to do with your screenplay after it's written:

What do you do with your screenplay after you've completed it?

First, you've got to find out whether it "works" or not; whether you should engrave it in stone or paper the walls with it. You need some kind of feedback to see whether you wrote what you set out to write.

At this moment you don't know whether it works or not; you can't see it; you're too close to it.

Hopefully your writing copy is fairly clean, so you can make a copy. Keep the original. Never, never, never give your original to anyone.

Give your script to two friends, close friends, friends you can trust, friends who will tell you the truth, friends who are not afraid to tell you: "I hate it. What you've written is weak and unreal, the characters flat and one-dimensional, the story contrived and predictable." Someone who will not be afraid to hurt your feelings.

You'll find most people won't tell you the truth about your script. They'll tell you what *they think* you want to hear: "It's good; I liked it! I really did. You've got some nice things in it. I think it's 'commercial,' " whatever that means! People mean well, but they don't realize they're hurting you more by not telling you the truth.

In Hollywood, nobody tells you what they really think; they tell you they liked it, but "it's not something we want to do at the present time"; or, "we have something like this in development."

That's not going to help you. You want someone to tell you what they really think about your script, so choose the people you give it to carefully.

After they've read it, listen to what they say. Don't defend what you've written, don't *pretend* to listen to what they say and leave feeling righteous, indignant, or hurt.

See whether they've caught the "intention" of what you wanted to write. Listen to their observations from the point of view that they *might be right*, not that they *are* right. They'll have observations, criticisms, suggestions, opinions, judgments. *Are* they right? Question them; press them on it. Do their suggestions or ideas make sense? Do they add to your screenplay? Enhance it? Go over the story with them. Find out what they like, dislike, what works for them, what doesn't.

You want the best script you can write. If you feel their suggestions can improve your screenplay, use them. Changes must be made from choice, and you must be comfortable with those changes. This is your story, and you'll know whether the changes work or not.

If you want to make any changes, make them. You've spent several months working on the script, so do it right. If you sell your material, you're going to have to make changes anyway; for the producer, director, and stars. Changes are changes; nobody likes them. But we all do them.

At this point, you still can't see your screenplay objectively. If you want another opinion "just in case," be prepared to get confused. If you give it to four people for example, they'll all disagree. One person will like the holdup of the Chase Manhattan Bank, another won't. One person will say they like the holdup, but not the *result* of the holdup (they either get away or don't); and the other one wonders why you didn't write a love story.

It doesn't work. Two people you can trust.

When you're satisfied with the script, you're ready to go to the typist. Your script must be clean, neat, and professional-looking. You can either type it yourself, or have it done by a professional typist. If you can, let a typist do the final copy. If you type it yourself you may find a tendency to "chip away" at it and change something that shouldn't be changed.

The *form* of your screenplay must be correct. Don't expect a typist to do it for you. It's not a typist's job. The pages you give the typist should be clean enough to read. Crossed-out lines, notations penciled in the margins, or pasted-up strips of paper are all okay. Just make sure the typist can read them. It will cost you anywhere from 95 cents to $1.25 per page to have it typed (at least at this writing).

Plan to spend about $100 in typing costs for the master copy (it will always be longer than your version; *do not* have the typist crowd the page to save a few dollars). It's a small amount to pay for the time spent writing it. The pleasure, the pain, and sheer hard work of writing has cost you far more than that.

Do not number your scenes. Final shooting scripts have numbers running down the left margin. They indicate scene breakdowns compiled by the *production manager*, not the writer. When a script is bought, and the director and cast are signed, a production manager is hired. The production manager and director will go over the script, scene by scene, shot by shot. Once locations are established, the production manager and his secretary will make a production board, a large foldout folio with each scene, interior or exterior, specifically notated on their cardboard strips. When the production board is completed and the scenes are notated and approved by the director, the production secretary types the numbers of each scene on each page for a shot-by-shot breakdown. These numbers are used to identify each shot, so when the film (maybe 3–500,000 feet of it) is processed, and catalogued, every piece of film will be identified. It is not the writer's job to number scenes.

A word about the title page. Many new or inexperienced writers feel they should include statements, registration, or copyright information, various quotes, dates, or whatever on the title page. They want to present "The Title," an original screenplay for an "epic production of a major motion picture for an all-star cast," by John Doe.

Don't do it. The title page is the title page. It should be simple and direct; "The Title" should be in the middle of the page, "a screenplay by John Doe" placed directly under it, and in the lower right hand corner your address or phone number. Several times, as head of the story department, I would receive material from new writers without any information about where I could reach them. Those scripts were held for two months, then dumped into the wastebasket.

You don't need to include copyright or registration information on the title page. But it is essential for you to protect your material.

There are three legal ways to claim ownership of your screenplay:

1. *Copyright* your screenplay: To do this, obtain copyright forms from the Library of Congress. Write to:

Registrar of Copyright
Library of Congress
Washington, D.C. 20540
or
Obtain copyright forms from your local Federal Building.
There is no charge for this service.

2. Place a copy of your screenplay in an envelope, and send it to yourself, special delivery, return receipt requested. Make sure the postmark shows clearly.

   When you receive the envelope, file it away. DO NOT OPEN IT!

3. Perhaps the easiest and most effective way to register your material is with the Writers Guild of America West or East. The Writers Guild provides registration service that "provides evidence of the writer's prior claim to authorship of the literary material involved and the date of its completion."

   At this writing, it costs a nonmember $10 and a member $4 to register material with the WGA. They take a clean copy of your screenplay, microfilm it, and store it in a safe place for ten years.

   Your receipt is "evidence," or "proof," you've written what you say you've written. If someone does plagiarize your material, your attorney will subpoena the Custodian of Records of the WGA and they will appear in your behalf.

   You may register your script by mail: Send a clean copy of your script with a check for the proper amount to the Registration Office:

   Writers Guild of America, West
   8955 Beverly Blvd.
   Los Angeles, CA 90048
   (213) 550-1000

or
Writers Guild of America, East
22 West 48th St.
New York, N.Y. 10036
(212) 575-5060

Several years ago, a friend of mine wrote a treatment for a movie about a competitive skier and sent it to Robert Redford. Redford's company returned the material with a "thanks, but no thanks" letter.

A year or so later she went to see a movie titled *Downhill Racer*, starring Robert Redford. She claimed it was her story.

She went to court and won a large settlement because she could prove "prior access"; her story was registered with the Writers Guild of America, and she had the "thanks, but no thanks" letter from Redford's company.

Nobody did anything "intentional" in this situation. They refused her idea, for whatever reason, and when they were looking for a subject for a film someone "had an idea" about a "downhill racer."

James Salter was called in and wrote an excellent screenplay; the film was made and released. As directed by Michael Ritchie, it's a fine film, one sadly neglected by its distributor and the viewing public.

Once you've got your "master copy" photocopy ten copies. A lot of people don't return material; especially with the rising cost of postage. (Sending a self-addressed, stamped envelope with your material simply lets the producer or story editor know that you're a novice screenwriter. Don't do it. The chances are it won't be returned anyway.) So: ten copies. You'll register one. That leaves nine. If you're fortunate to get an agent to represent you, he'll want five copies immediately. That leaves you with four.

Make sure your screenplay is bound with paper fasteners; do not submit it loose. Put a simple cover on it, a cover that lends itself to the screenplay. Do not use a fancy, embossed leatherette cover. Make sure your script is on 8½ × 11 paper, and not 8½ × 14, legal size, the way they do it in England.

You've got "one shot" with your script, so make it count. One shot means this: At Cinemobile, every submission received was logged in a card file and cross-indexed by title and author. The material was read, evaluated, and written up in synopsis form. The reader's comments were carefully registered, then filed away.

If you submit your screenplay to a studio or production company, and they read it and reject it, and then you decide to rewrite it and resubmit it, chances are it won't be read. The reader will read the original synopsis and return it to you. Change the title, or use a pseudonym. No one reads the same material twice.

Do not send a synopsis of your script along with your material; it will not be read. If it is, it will be to your disadvantage. All our decisions were usually based on the reader's comments. If the synopsis had an interesting premise, we glanced through the first ten pages and then made a decision.

Some story editors at studios, networks, or production companies will accept unsolicited material only if you sign a release that permits them to read it. For the most part, studios will return your screenplay unopened and unread. Like insurance companies, they've been "burned" by plagiarism suits a few too many times and they don't want to deal with it. I don't blame them.

Then how do you "get it" to people? Since most people in Hollywood don't accept unsolicited material—that is, they don't accept material unless it's submitted through an authorized literary agent, an agent who has signed the Artists-

Managers Agreement drawn up by the WGA—the question then becomes: How do you get an agent?

I hear that question over and over again. If you're going to sell your script for $250,000 and have Robert Redford and Faye Dunaway star in it, you need a literary agent. So, how do you get an agent?

First, you must have a completed screenplay. An outline, or treatment, doesn't work. Then, contact the Writers Guild of America, West or East. Ask them, by mail or phone, to send you the list of agents who are signatory to the Artists-Managers Agreement. They'll send you a list of scores of agents. Those agents who are willing to read unsolicited material from new writers are indicated.

List several of them. Contact them by mail or phone; ask if they would be interested in reading a screenplay by a new writer. Give your background. Sell yourself.

Most of them will say "no." Try some more. They'll say "no," too. Try some more.

People are always looking for material. That's the irony and truth. There is a dearth of salable material in Hollywood. The opportunities for new screenwriters are enormous.

Many times you'll talk to the agent's secretary. Sometimes they'll read your screenplay; if they like it they'll recommend it to the agent. Let anyone who wants to read your script read it. A good script does not go unfound.

Good material does not get away from the readers in Hollywood. They can spot potential movie material within ten pages. If your script is good and worthy of production, it's going to be found. "How" is another matter.

It's a survival process. Your screenplay is entering the raging current of the Hollywood River, and like salmon swimming upstream to spawn, only a few make it.

Last year some 15,840 screenplays were registered with

the Writers Guild of America, West, in Los Angeles. The registration office receives some 100 submissions a day. Two-thirds of everything written are screenplays. That means approximately 66 people are registering a screenplay every day. That's 1,320 scripts in one month—15,840 a year!

Do you know how many movies are made by studios and independent production companies each year? Between eighty and ninety. And the number of studio productions is *decreasing*, while the number of people writing screenplays is *increasing*.

Figure it out. Keep your dreams and reality separate. They're two different worlds.

If an agent likes your material, he still may not be able to sell it. But he will be able to show your screenplay as a sample of your writing ability. If a producer or story editor likes your work, you may be able to get a "development deal" from a studio or producer to write an original, or adapt one of their ideas or books into a screenplay. Everybody's looking for writers, no matter what "they" say.

Give the agent three to six weeks to read your material. If you don't receive a reply from him or her within that period of time, call.

If you submit your script to a large, well-known agency, like William Morris, or ICM, the established agents will ignore it. But they have readers and trainee agents there and they might read it.

If you're fortunate, you might find someone who likes your work and wants to represent you.

Who is the best agent?

The agent who likes *your* work and wants to represent you.

If you contact eight agents, you'll be lucky to find one who likes it. You can submit your script to more than one agent at a time.

A literary agent gets a 10-percent commission of whatever he or she sells.

What kind of a deal can you expect to make if someone wants to buy your screenplay?

Prices for a screenplay vary from Writers Guild minimum to $400,000 or more. The Writers Guild minimum is broken down into two categories: a high-budget movie that costs more than $1 million to make and a low-budget film that costs less than $1 million. At this writing, the WGA minimum for a high-budget film is $20,821; for a low budget, $11,211. These minimums will increase each time a new contract is negotiated.

An "eyeball" price for a screenplay is 5 percent of the budget. If you sell the script, you'll probably receive a "percentage of the profits," at least on paper. You'll get anywhere from 2½ to 5 percent of the producer's net, whatever you can get.

If someone wants to buy your script for $25,000 they will probably *option* it for a year. With an option, someone pays you for the exclusive right to get a "deal" or raise financing for a certain period of time, usually a year. The option price will usually be 5–10 percent of the purchase price. With a purchase price of $25,000 you'll receive a $2,500 option.

Let's take a one-year period.

You have a $2,500 option on your script, leaving a balance due you of $22,500—the $25,000 purchase price minus the $2,500 option money.

If a *production-distribution* agreement is made with a "money source," you'll receive the balance in full, or a certain amount applied against the total. A production-distribution agreement is when a financially responsible money source—a studio, or production funding company—agrees to finance and distribute the movie. When the p/d agreement is reached, they may make an additional payment, and perhaps pay the balance of the purchase price on the "first day of principal photography." That is, the first day of shooting. That may be more than a year after you receive your option money. This is a standard-type "step-deal" in Hollywood. The money numbers may vary, the procedure will not.

If you do get an offer on your script, let someone represent you. Either an agent or an attorney.

You can obtain an option for a book or novel just like a screenplay. If you want to adapt a book or novel, you must obtain the motion-picture and theatrical rights to it.

To find out if the material is available, call the publisher of the hardbound edition. Ask, either by mail or phone, for the subsidiary rights department. Ask if the motion-picture and theatrical rights are available. If they are, they'll tell you or refer you to the literary agent who represents the author. Contact them. The agent will tell you whether the rights are available or not.

If you decide to adapt the material without obtaining the motion-picture rights, you might find you've been wasting your time; the rights are not available, someone owns them. If you can find out who has the rights, they might be willing to read your screenplay. Or, they might not.

If you want to adapt the material simply as an exercise for yourself, do it. Just be sure you know what you're doing so you're not wasting your time.

It costs so much to make a movie today that everyone wants to minimize the risk; that's why money paid to a writer is termed "front money," or "risk money."

No one likes to take a risk. And the motion-picture business is one of the biggest crap shoots around. No one knows whether a film is going to "go through the roof," like *Star Wars* or *Saturday Night Fever*. People are reluctant to put up a lot of front money. Do you know anyone who spends money easily? Including yourself? Studios, production companies, and independent producers are no exception.

Option money comes out of the producer's pocket; they want to minimize the risks. Don't expect a lot of money for your material the first time out. It doesn't work that way.

Most first screenplays don't sell. John Milius wrote his first screenplay several years ago, a piece called *The Last Resort*.

It still hasn't sold. Nobody wants to buy it, and Milius doesn't care to rewrite it. Yet it clearly reveals John Milius' unique gift for telling a story visually. Milius is a "natural" filmmaker, like Spielberg, or Kubrick, men "born to film." Though unsold, *The Last Resort* began his career.

There are a few exceptions. Bob Getchell's *Alice Doesn't Live Here Anymore* was a first screenplay. Rob Thompson's *Hearts of the West* was a first effort that he managed to get to Tony Bill, long a champion of the new writer, and the movie got made.

These are the exceptions, not the rule.

When you really get down to it, you're writing your screenplay for yourself first, for money second.

Only a handful of well-known and established writers in Hollywood get enormous sums of money for their screenplays. There are more than 4,600 members of the Writers Guild, West, and only about 200 are employed to write screenplays. And less than a handful earn six figures a year. Those that do, earn every penny of it.

Don't set up unreal expectations for yourself.

Just write your screenplay.

Then worry about how much money you're going to make.

18

A Personal Note

Wherein we comment:

Everybody's a writer.

That's what you'll find out. Everybody you tell about your screenplay will have a suggestion, a comment, or a better idea about it. Then, they'll tell you about the great idea *they* have for a screenplay.

It's one thing to *say* you're going to write a screenplay, it's another *to do* it.

Don't make judgments about what you've written. It might take years for you to "see" your script objectively. If at all. Judgments of "good" or "bad," or comparisons between this and that are meaningless within the creative experience.

It is what it is.

As a native of Los Angeles I've been around the Hollywood film industry all my life. As a child, I was up for a part in *Gone With the Wind*; at twelve, I was on the set of Frank Capra's *State of the Union,* with Spencer Tracy and Katharine Hepburn; as a teenager, my "club" at Hollywood High was the model for the gang that hunted James Dean in *Rebel Without a Cause.*

Hollywood is a "dream factory"; a town of talkers. Go to any of the various hangouts around town and you'll hear people talking about the scripts they're going to write, the movies they're going to produce, the deals they're going to make.

It's all talk.

Action is character, right? What a person *does* is what he *is*, not what he says.

Everybody's a writer.

There is a tendency in Hollywood to "second-guess" the writer; the studio, the producer, the director, and the star will make changes in the script that will "improve" it. Most people in Hollywood assume they're "larger" than the original material. "*They*" know what has to be done to "make it better." Directors do this all the time.

A film director can take a great script and make a great film. Or, he can take a great script and make a terrible film. But he can't take a terrible script and make a great film. No way.

Only a few film directors know how to improve a screenplay by visually tightening the story line. They can take a wordy dialogue scene of three or four pages, condense it into a tense and dramatic three-minute scene that "works" with five lines of dialogue, three looks, somebody lighting a cigarette, and an insert of a clock on the wall. Sidney Lumet did this in *Network*. He took a 160-page screenplay, beautifully written and constructed, and visually tightened it into an excellent 120-minute film that captures the integrity of the script by Paddy Chayefsky.

That's the exception, not the rule.

Most directors in Hollywood have no story sense at all. They'll second-guess the writer, making changes in the story line that weaken and distort it, and eventually a lot of money is spent making a lousy film that nobody wants to see.

In the long run of course, everybody loses: the studios lose money, the director adds a "flop" to his "track record," and the writer takes the rap for writing a poor screenplay.

Everybody's a writer.

Some people will complete their screenplays. Others won't. Writing is hard work, a day-by-day job, and a professional writer is someone who sets out to achieve a goal and then does it. Just like life. Writing is a personal responsibility; either you do it or you don't. And then there's the old "natural law" about survival and evolution.

There are no "overnight success stories" in Hollywood. Like the saying goes, "The overnight success took 15 years to happen."

Believe it. It's true.

Professional success is measured by persistence and determination. The motto of the McDonald's Corporation is summed up in their poster called "Press On":

Nothing in the world can take the place
of persistence.
Talent will not; nothing is more common
than unsuccessful men with talent.
Genius will not; unrewarded genius
is almost a proverb.
Education will not;
the world is full of educated derelicts.
Persistence and determination alone
are omnipotent.

When you complete your screenplay, you've accomplished a tremendous achievement. You've taken an idea, expanded it into a dramatic or comedic story line, then sat down and spent several weeks or months writing it. From inception through completion. It's a satisfying and rewarding experience. You did what you set out to do.

Wear that proudly.

Talent is God's gift; either you've got it, or you don't. But that doesn't interfere with the experience of writing.

Writing brings its own rewards. Enjoy them.

Pass it on.

Index